NO
ROOM
FOR
SMALL
DREAMS

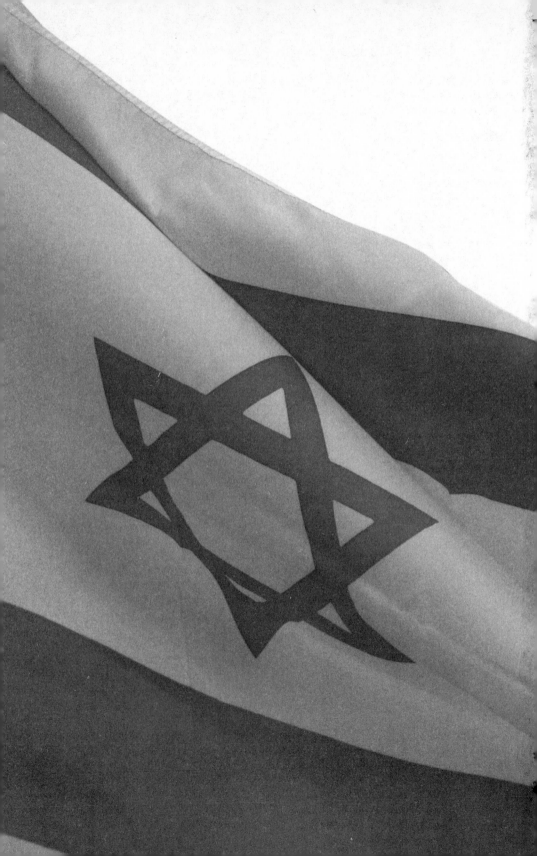

NO
ROOM
FOR
SMALL
DREAMS

COURAGE, IMAGINATION,
AND THE MAKING OF
MODERN ISRAEL

SHIMON
PERES

CUSTOM
HOUSE

The Peres family would like to thank Dylan Loewe and his team at
West Wing Writers for their assistance.

FIRST EDITION

Designed by William Ruoto

Library of Congress Cataloging-in-Publication Data has been applied for.

ISBN 978-0-06-256144-2

17 18 19 20 21   LSC   10 9 8 7 6 5 4 3 2 1

To the next generation of leaders, in Israel and around the world

CONTENTS

Timeline ix

Introduction xi

CHAPTER 1:
The Call to Service 1

CHAPTER 2:
Independence, Alliance, and the Fight for Security 35

CHAPTER 3:
The Legend and Legacy of Dimona 81

CHAPTER 4:
Operation Entebbe and the Virtue of Daring 107

CHAPTER 5:
Building the Start-up Nation 145

CHAPTER 6:
The Pursuit of Peace 173

Epilogue 221

Afterword 227

SHIMON PERES: NEARLY SEVEN
DECADES OF PUBLIC SERVICE

1923:   Born in Vishneva, Poland, on August 2

1934:   Immigrated to the land of Israel

1938:   Enrolled at Ben-Shemen Youth Village

1945:   Elected Secretary-General of HaNoar HaOved

1947:   Recruited to the Haganah by David Ben-Gurion

1948–1949:   Head of the Naval Service

1949–1952:   Director of the Ministry of Defense Mission in the United States

1953–1959:   Director General, Ministry of Defense

1959–2007:   Member of the Knesset

1959–1965:   Deputy Minister of Defense

1969:   Minister of Immigrant Absorption

1970–1974:   Minister of Transportation and Postal Services

1974:   Minister of Information

1974–1977:   Minister of Defense

1977–1992:   Chairman of the Israeli Labor Party

1984–1986:   Prime Minister of the State of Israel

1986–1988:   Deputy Prime Minister and Minister of Foreign Affairs

1988–1990:   Deputy Prime Minister and Minister of Finance

1992–1995:   Minister of Foreign Affairs

1995–1996:   Prime Minister of the State of Israel

TIMELINE

1999–2001:   Minister of Regional Cooperation

2001–2002:   Deputy Prime Minister and Minister of Foreign Affairs

2005:   Vice Prime Minister

2006:   Minister for the Development of the Negev and Galilee

2007–2014:   Ninth President of the State of Israel

Your father is like the wind," our mother used to say, "You will never be able to stop him or hold him back." And right she was.

In private, Shimon Peres was our father. In public, he was one of the founding fathers of the State of Israel. He dedicated his life to a never-ending masterpiece: building a better future. The tools of his trade included faith, perseverance, resilience, and the ability to learn—to change and to grow. But his greatest tool of all, always, was hope. He used hope to plant foundations deep into hard ground, to stand sturdy and fearless on shaky scaffolding, to reach up, as high as only dreams can take us, to discover a previously obscured rung on a heretofore unrevealed ladder—and then foresee the next.

His life was as improbable and extraordinary as his beloved home. He believed that achieving peace and making Israel a better place were both part of creating a more harmonious, prosperous, and generous world, and that there was no higher aspiration a person could hold than this.

Our father used to say: "Count the number of dreams you have and compare them with the number of achievements you've had. If you have more dreams than achievements, then you are still young." He wrote this book in his final year, as a gift to the next generation, to those young of age and young of heart. He wished to pass on his battered and trusty toolbox so that we may all learn from his yesterdays and continue the work of building a better tomorrow. In accordance with his wishes, we are grateful to share it with you.

TSVIA, YONI, AND CHEMI

CHAPTER 1

THE CALL TO SERVICE

I was eleven years old the first time I saw the place, tucked away and surrounded by trees. The simple house belonged to my aunt and uncle, who built it themselves after settling in the land of Israel. It was 1934, a time when the area was home to only a few thousand Jews; its roads remained unpaved, the land largely unsettled.

As we got closer, I realized that the trees were not a kind I'd ever seen before; they were orange groves, planted by hand. My older brother Gigi and I set off at once, racing up and down the perfectly placed rows, each tree bearing more than a hundred plump, bright fruits. The remaining white blossoms filled the air with an enchanting fragrance.

In my mind I was suddenly back in my small Jewish village—back in the "shtetl," as they were called—back to the moment I'd first seen an orange, back to a place so very far away.

Our shtetl was known as Vishneva. It sat near the border between Poland and Russia, a strip of land surrounded by forest that existed in a seemingly permanent state of winter. There were often weeks on end where bitterly frigid winds would whip through the narrow birch trees, sweeping unforgivingly against the patrons in the market. Even during the summer, it felt like we rarely saw the sun. And yet despite the cold and isolation there was a warmth and magic to the shtetl, a culture of kindness and community. We had found, in each other, a place to belong.

We lived a simple life: there were only three roads, each lined with bare wooden houses. There was no running water and no electricity. But there was a train station, just three miles away, and from its travelers and its shipments we got a glimpse—and a taste—of the world beyond the forest.

I still remember that powerful moment, that first orange. My parents had taken me to the home of their friends, where a large group had already gathered. A young man had arrived, recently returned from the land of Israel, and was regaling the crowd with grand stories of a distant land. He spoke of endless sunshine and exotic culture, of patches of desert with fruit-bearing trees, of tough, tanned Jews who worked with their hands and fought with them, too. When he finished, he turned to a box behind him and lifted it for those gathered to see. There was an audible gasp in the room. There was a ceremony to his presentation, a formality that suggested this had been done many times before. One by one, each person in the room chose a package from the box, delicately undoing the parchment wrapping to reveal a ripe Jaffa orange, picked straight from the tree. When it was my turn, I was slow and deliberate, nervous that I might do something wrong. I held the orange to my nose, breathing in my first smell of citrus. It was truly extraordinary—in color, in fragrance, in taste—as otherworldly as anything a young boy could have imagined. It was so much more than a piece of fruit; it was a symbol of my hopes and aspirations.

My family had lived in the area for several generations. And, indeed, the area had, for hundreds of years, been a place for Jews to call home. But despite its simple beauty, neither of my parents considered Vishneva their permanent home. They saw it more as a way station, one of many stops over thousands of years along the road back to our homeland. The land of Israel was not just the dream of my parents; it was the animating purpose of so many people we knew. It seemed that at every gathering, the conversation turned to talk of going to Zion, of leaving the shtetl we loved behind, of joining the pioneers who were reclaiming our land. We spoke often of Theodor Herzl, the founder of the Zionist movement, who argued that the future of the Jewish people depended on the existence of a Jewish state, one bonded together not just by religion but by language and nationality. "Let them give us sovereignty over a piece of the earth's surface, just sufficient for the needs of our people. Then we will do the rest."

Herzl's dream had become my own. I thought of my family as people living contently, yet in exile. We spoke Hebrew, we thought in Hebrew, and we eagerly read the news that came from Mandatory Palestine, the British-controlled territory (or "mandate") that included our ancient homeland. There was a collective longing—a yearning to return—that came with a powerful grip. There were times when it made me feel as though I were in purgatory between a faraway past and an imminent future. The closer to that future we came, the more unbearable the delay felt.

Despite that desire to journey onward, my memories of childhood are endless and fond. My mother, Sara, was brilliant and loving, a librarian by training and a devotee to Russian literature. There were few things in life that brought her more joy than reading, a joy she shared with me. I grew up to become a man of books, but I started as a boy of books, reading next to my mother. There was a loving challenge to it—to try to keep up with her—if only for the discussion to follow. My father, Yitzhak (known as Getzel), was warm and generous, a lumber merchant like his father before him. He was a man full of energy and kindness, both doting and diligent. He emboldened me always, and beamed at my achievements. His love gave me confidence, and my confidence gave me the ability to fly. I felt profoundly blessed.

My parents raised me without many boundaries or limits, never telling me what to do, always trusting that my curiosity would lead me down the right path. In my youngest years, when I decided to put on shows and make speeches in front of my parents and their friends, I received nothing but encouragement. Sometimes I would offer up impressions (there were a few people around town whose voices and mannerisms I had perfected). Other times I would deliver fully formed addresses about the nature of Zionism or the relative virtues of my most favorite writers. To the adults, this made me the precocious young boy with a bright future ahead. To me, it felt like the beginning of something bigger. But to my schoolmates, it made me something of an outcast, the one so clearly unlike the others. What I was, in fact, was what I have remained: at ninety-three, I am still that curious boy, enamored of hard questions, eager to dream, and unbowed by the doubt of others.

My parents helped shaped the man I became, but it was my grandfather, Rabbi Zvi Meltzer, whom I admired most deeply, and with whom I formed one of the most important bonds in my life. He was a stocky man who somehow always looked tall. Having attended the finest yeshiva in Europe, he served as the shtetl's chief rabbi. If Zionism was the center of our civic lives, Judaism was the center of our moral lives. He was the authority figure from whom my family took our direction and, because of his position and his exceptional mind, the community leader to whom the entire shtetl turned for guidance and wisdom.

I felt especially lucky, not just to have such an important figure in the family, but because he gave me special attention. He was the first to teach me the history of the Jewish people, and the first to acquaint me with the Torah. I would join him each Sabbath at the synagogue, and followed intently the weekly reading. Like other Jews, I considered Yom Kippur, the Jewish day of atonement, the highest of holidays. It had special resonance for me, though, not just for its own significance, but because I would get to hear my grandfather sing. Only on that day would he serve as our cantor, his wonderful voice booming out the hauntingly beautiful prayer of *Kol Nidre*. It would move me to the depths of my soul and I would hide under his prayer shawl, the only place I felt safe on such a serious day. From the darkness of my hiding place, I would ask God to forgive the transgressors and have mercy on every man, as he himself had sown the seeds of weakness.

In his image, and from his teachings, I became strictly religious myself as a child, much more so than my parents. I came to believe that my obligation was to serve God through His commandments, and that no exception could be tolerated. My parents didn't fully appreciate the depths of my commitment until the day my father brought a radio home, the first in Vishneva. In his excitement to show my mother how it worked, he turned it on during the Sabbath—a time of rest and contemplation during which Judaism forbids certain actions, including those required to switch on a radio. I was furious.

I threw it to the ground in a fit of overzealous righteousness, breaking it irreparably as though the fate of humanity depended on my doing so. I am grateful that they were forgiving.

When I wasn't at home or in synagogue, I would try to hitch a carriage ride to the train station; it was from here that people would begin the long journey that would take them to our ancient homeland. The whole town would gather in loud celebration, wishing farewell to their neighbors in bittersweet fashion. I watched with admiration, joining in the cheering and reverent joy, but I always returned home with a tinge of sadness, wondering if my turn would ever really come.

In time, circumstances required us to leave. By the early 1930s, my father's business had been destroyed by anti-Semitic taxes levied against Jewish enterprises. Left with nothing, he decided it was time to depart. In 1932, he set off on his journey to Mandatory Palestine by himself, a pioneer in his own right, eager to get settled and prepare for our arrival. It was another two long years—a lifetime for an impatient child—until he sent word that he was ready to receive us. I was eleven years old when my mother came to Gigi and me and told us the time had come.

We loaded our possessions into the back of a horse-drawn cart and set off on the ride to the train station. The cart creaked as it bounced frenetically over the many rocks in the road. My mother didn't enjoy it, but for my brother and me, every jolt was a joy—a reminder that the great adventure was already well under way. We were dressed in thick wool jackets and heavy winter shoes that we would soon no longer need.

When we arrived at the station, there were dozens of people waiting to send us off with well-wishes and prayers. My grandfather was one of them. Given his age and centrality to the community, he had chosen to stay in Vishneva. He was the only thing I knew I would miss about my hometown. I watched him say goodbye to my mother and brother on the platform, and waited for him to face me, not knowing what I'd say. His large frame loomed over me as I looked up toward his eyes through his thick, graying beard. They had tears in them. He placed a hand on my shoulder, then bent down to meet my gaze.

"Promise me one thing," he said, with the same commanding voice I had come to know so well.

"Anything, *Zaydeh*."

"Promise me you'll always remain Jewish."

My grandfather's life ended in Vishneva. The Nazis marched through the forest and into the village square only a few years after I left, gathering up the Jews to meet a horrific fate. My grandfather was forced into our modest wooden synagogue along with most of his congregation, while the Nazis boarded the doors. What terror they must have experienced, I cannot comprehend—the first moment the smoke poured in through the cracks of the door; the crackling sound that would have made them realize the building had been set ablaze from outside. I am told that as the flames grew violent, as they engulfed our most cherished place of worship, my grandfather donned his prayer shawl, the same one I had hidden under during Yom Kippur, and chanted a final prayer—a last moment of stoic dignity before the fire stole his words and his breath and his life, along with all the others.

The Jews who remained were rounded up, house to house, pulled from their hiding places, snatched from their lives. They were forced to watch as the shtetl was destroyed, as though a tornado had torn through the area, but with precision and intent. They were marched to the train station, through the cruel rubble, past the fiery grave. The same tracks that had started me on the journey to my homeland would take them to the death camps instead.

I hadn't known, when we boarded the train for Mandatory Palestine, when it lurched to a start and I waved good-bye through the window, that I would never see my grandfather again. I can still hear his voice every time a cantor chants the *Kol Nidre*. I can still feel his spirit every time I face a hard choice.

. . .

In 1934, our journey to Mandatory Palestine took us south to the Mediterranean Sea, which seemed to stretch endlessly that first time I saw it. We boarded a steamship for a several-day voyage through mostly calm waters. I was convinced that the absence of squall and rough seas was a sign from above. From the deck of the ship, enveloped in all directions by dramatic blue skies, I could feel the gentle heat of the sun unimpeded by clouds. It was as though my world had been repainted and reheated to animate my dreams.

On our final day at sea, I awoke to the sound of the ship's air horn. The captain was alerting passing boats to our arrival and, in his way, announcing it to the passengers, as well. Gigi and I scrambled out of bed and ran up the stairs to the top deck, where we hoped to see the first glimpse of our new life. A group of passengers had gathered already, shouting and singing with delight. I made my way through the crowd until I was standing at the railing, with nothing and no one blocking my view.

Outstretched before me was the magnificent shoreline of Jaffa. The sea seemed to be composed of all shades of blue, the bright sapphire of the deep waters dancing with the iridescent turquoise in the shallows as they lapped against the perfect white sand beach. Beyond the bay I could see a hill in the distance—the heart of a grand and ancient city. The collection of stone buildings that surrounded the promontory seemed to be standing at attention and on guard. Behind them, a slender clock stretched for the sky.

I didn't know much about Jaffa before I arrived, only that it was an ancient city that was mentioned in the Bible. Now, as it came into view, I could see a texture and vibrancy that could have been gleaned only firsthand. There were large crowds of people in red fezzes and checkered headdresses. Some had gathered together to enjoy the bright morning, playing with small children as the sea breeze moved through their loosely fitting robes. Others had boarded boats to meet us in the heart of the bay. Most of these were filled with people offering to sell passengers things we had never tasted. They offered us jars of lemonade over crushed ice, and dates harvested from the palm trees I had known only from my aunt's pictures. Some of the boats had been chartered by Jews, who were picking up passengers right there where we anchored.

As I scanned the boats looking for my father, I noticed scores of local Jews whom I barely resembled. In perpetually gray Vishneva, every Jew I knew was incredibly pale. To be among these men who were tanned by the sun and chiseled by the hard work of cultivating the land was to be among heroes. I wanted nothing more than to join them, to become one of them.

Eventually I spotted my father standing at the front of a small Arab fishing boat, enthusiastically waving at my brother and me, so much tanner than when last I had seen him. Beside him stood the captain of the vessel, a tall Arab man dressed in wide, flowing pants with accordion creases. We leapt into the boat and greeted our father with two years of unspent love. To us he gave the same. As we made our way to shore, I could feel the sun's warmth beating down through my thick winter jacket. I closed my eyes and imagined the soft heat was my own personal welcome, a welcome from a sun that had been biding its time until my arrival. The moment I stepped out of the boat and onto the land, I knew I had found my way home.

The land of Israel suited me well. Over time, I felt like I was sloughing off my old life, as though Vishneva had been my cocoon and now I had grown wings. I stopped wearing jackets and ties, trading them in for short sleeves instead. I watched my skin darken under the clearest blue skies, and never felt more like a true child of Israel than when I came home with a sunburn. I loved books with intense fervor and interest, but now I read them under a sycamore tree in the park or on the sands at the edge of the sea.

. . .

On July 15, 2007, I was sworn in as Israel's ninth president. I was eighty-three years old. It was the culmination of a career that spanned the life of the state itself, a final opportunity to serve the people through government. Standing on the stage, taking the oath of office, it was Vishneva that occupied my mind, a reminder of where my journey had started. I had an endless imagination as an eleven-year-old boy, but even in my most ambitious dreams, I never thought that I would find myself at such a moment.

At a celebration the evening of my swearing in, a young man I'd never met approached me, launching straight into conversation with an unabashed Israeli frankness I couldn't help but admire.

"Mr. President, with due respect, after such a long career, why would you keep working at your age?"

"Why do I serve?" I asked. "I suppose I never considered the alternative."

It was the truth. As long as I could recall, Zionism had been the center of my identity, and service to it a requirement for its success. In my eighties, that service led me to the presidency, after six decades in Israeli politics. But as I came of age as a young man in Mandatory Palestine, the service I imagined was not work in government; it was work in the fields, work settling the land, work creating a new kind of community. I wanted nothing more than to be a kibbutznik.

The first settlement known as a kibbutz was called Degania, established in the Jordan Valley in 1910 by a group of young pioneers who had fled Europe. They had come with grand plans, not just to build settlements, but to make real the dream that was Zionism. The kibbutzim were, first and foremost, agricultural settlements, places where people worked to the bone, tilling the rocky soil and draining wretched swamps. It was the pioneers who were working every day to make the uninhabitable bloom. In due time, Degania inspired others, and the barren lands of the Jezreel and Jordan Valleys became dotted with flourishing communities. There were around thirty kibbutzim when I immigrated to Israel, and many more in time. In the harshest conditions, they reshaped the landscape with palm trees and field crops and orchards and livestock. They made the desert beautiful and bountiful, and in doing so, convinced us of the limitless potential we could summon among us. In the years before statehood, we had strong leadership and were building the foundations for state institutions and a government. During that time—and out of necessity—it was the kibbutzim that became our most central institutions, not just because of their delicate harvests or elegant ideology, but because they took on the essential responsibilities: managing settlements and immigration and organizing our defense. And while each kibbutz had its own unique characteristics, they all organized themselves around the same central vision. In their pursuit of the Zionist dream, the pioneers had also tried to reimagine a new kind of society, one built on equality and cooperation, on justice and fairness, on collective ownership and communal living.

I enjoyed my life in Tel Aviv, the afternoons spent riding my bicycle down the streets, counting the new buildings, cataloging the daily progress of construction. But it was the kibbutzim in the distance that captured my heart. I had joined the youth movement at my high school, through which I had met and learned from the Jewish nation's greatest pioneers. At school, we studied—but in the youth movement, we dreamed. I had become convinced, having spent so much of my childhood lionizing the pioneers, that there was no more essential a mission, no higher a calling than to join them. I wanted to trade the noise of the city for the quiet of the fields—to be a part of the quest to transform the land. Over time, our group leader, Elhanan Yishai, came to understand the path I sought to travel and, in his kindness, chose me as someone to help.

"I think you should consider Ben-Shemen," he said to me, during a conversation that would change the course of my life. It was the first time I had heard its name.

Ben-Shemen Youth Village was many things to many people.

Founded in 1927 by Dr. Siegfried Lehmann, a German physician and educator, it was—and remains—the most wonderful place I have ever known.

It was, first and foremost, a place to call home, including for the brave and weakened children who had been orphaned in Europe, and yet somehow made their way to Mandatory Palestine alone. But it was so much more than that. It was both an intellectual center of Zionism and a place to learn the most practical applications of its tenets. It was a place where boys and girls could acquire the skills required to settle the arid land: how to herd sheep and milk the goats and the cows; how to press seeds into the hard, salty soil in a way that would give them nourishment; the proper way to sharpen and swing a scythe. It was also a place where boys and girls were trained to be soldiers, knowing that Zionism would surely require a fight. Students learned how to shoot, how to fight, how to navigate by the stars. But most of all, they would learn the values that kibbutz life represented: how to work together as equals, how to build and sustain a community over time. It was a place that turned children into leaders. Ben-Shemen had just accepted a large wave of children from Europe, and its leaders were hoping to match them with others who, having emigrated from Europe themselves, could help the new arrivals adjust to a very different life.

Before I had the chance to respond, Elhanan injected a final piece of information. "You don't have to go," he said. "But I want you to know I already recommended you, and because I know of your family's financial situation, I also applied for a scholarship on your behalf." I must have looked truly stunned.

"They want you, Shimon," he said with a smile, "and they will cover the costs. So if you want to do this, the decision is yours."

I leapt from my chair and raced straight to my house to tell my mother and father. I didn't even ask for their permission. I just told them my plan and my hopes with all of the passion and impatience of a fifteen-year-old boy. This, I was certain, was my destiny. I think they thought so, too.

I arrived at Ben-Shemen in 1938, brimming with opinions and eager to learn. I remember first walking through its entrance and into the courtyard, a small square surrounded by modest one-story buildings. There were two beautiful oak trees in the heart of the courtyard, old giants that must have borne witness to centuries of history. Under them stood a small group of children gathered around what looked like their teacher, listening intently as she discussed the day's lesson.

I was assigned to a spare wooden cabin at the end of a narrow dirt path where I lived happily with two other boys. There were times, at first glance, when it must have looked like a summer camp. We told jokes and played pranks and sang songs by the fire. We went on long, winding hikes through the neighboring foothills and played all sorts of games while we worked through our chores. It was the first time, and first place, where I truly made friends. In Tel Aviv, I was an outsider. At Ben-Shemen I was popular.

And yet despite the camaraderie and the occasional mischief, we were all keenly aware that we were part of a mission—something far bigger than ourselves. We weren't just living on the frontier of Jewish history; we were shaping it with our hands. With every seed we planted and every crop we harvested, we were extending the reach of our dreams. This was the harsh land on which we were going to rebuild the Jewish state—and it fell to us to tame it, to make sure it could support many millions of others. What kind of security can we provide to our people, we were often reminded, if we can't fill their bellies once they come? So we had to prepare.

By day, we worked the fields or studied in our classrooms. By night, we stood guard. It was not unusual for Arabs in the neighboring villages to fire their weapons at us or try to pilfer our food and supplies. I had been appointed commander of one of the guard posts, a reinforced concrete structure at the edge of the village. The sun having set, I would crawl up its wrought-iron ladder and position myself as a lookout, my back against one wall, my rifle at my side. Each time, I hoped for a quiet evening—but there were many times when the village was shot at, many nights when I had to exchange fire with the darkness.

Each night of my posting I would pass by the Gelmans' house. Mr. Gelman was our carpentry teacher, and oftentimes I would see him in the front yard, sawing away at a long board of wood. Sometimes I would see his wife tending the garden, watering her flowers or checking the progress of her tomatoes. "Hello," I would call out with a wave.

On one particular night, however, there was someone I didn't recognize standing barefoot in their doorway. Her long brown hair was pulled back and braided, revealing piercing eyes and a porcelain face, a beauty like none I had ever seen. We made eye contact just for a moment, and with the slightest of smiles, I was hers. It was as though she had destroyed me and rebuilt me in an instant. Her name was Sonia. She was Gelman's second daughter, and had spent her whole life growing up in the village. Each night I would see her, always without shoes, a lawn mower by her side. I was mesmerized.

In time I would find the courage to speak to her. But she was not impressed by me. I did my best: I read her poems, even chapters of Karl Marx, but nothing seemed to break through. Not until the day I asked her to accompany me to a young cucumber field. There was something about the perfume of the cucumbers, the romance of nature, that must have finally worked. She looked at me differently, finally—the way I had been looking at her.

Sonia was my first and only love. I would come to find a young woman who was both gentle and firm, and, in every way, a source of great wisdom and strength. Sonia let me dream, but kept me grounded. She believed in me and supported me as I chased my wildest visions. But she never let me get ahead of myself. She was my compass and my conscience, in one. In all of the world, there could not have been another person more deserving of my love, and somehow—for some reason—she seemed ready to love me, too.

This was Ben-Shemen. It was a place where we learned by day and defended by night. A place where we could be ourselves and chase our purpose. A place where soul mates waited for you a short walk down the road.

It was also a place of great political drama. It was there that I first started to refine my political opinions, and the first place I had the chance to put them to good use. Indeed, for all that we learned from our teachers at Ben-Shemen, there were few things more formative than what we did in the shadows. Ben-Shemen was home to a number of political youth movements, organizations where students would debate the future of the Jewish people, the necessity of a Jewish state, and the strategy required to create one. But this kind of political activity was officially forbidden on the grounds, so any such debates would take place at night, in secret whispers and impassioned pleas. These were the conversations of a generation—the youngest generation—rooted in a sense that it was our own future we were trying to build, that what we spoke were more than words. We felt as though our mission was greater than securing a homeland, that it was our job to imagine a new society. This was the driving concept behind the kibbutz system, and the idea that we had so firmly embraced. And perhaps because the stakes were so high, and because our role felt so central, our debates were often quite heated.

There were plenty of disagreements among us, despite our shared aspirations. Some of the leaders were Stalinists, people who demanded ideological collectivism in their kibbutzim and saw a Jewish state as a mechanism for greater discipline and order. They wanted to replicate the Soviet system. I, on the other hand, believed that Stalin had perverted the teachings of Marx, that his style of government was anathema to the socialist ideal. Rather than replicate his system of government—or any other—I believed we needed one that was uniquely our own, one that reflected a national ethos based on the tenets of Jewish morality. As Herzl had once said, "It is true that we aspire to our ancient land. But what we want in that ancient land is a new blossoming of the Jewish spirit."

I was increasingly a key player in our secret gatherings, no longer the outsider. The early experiences of the youth movement transformed me, shaping how I saw the world and, increasingly, where I saw myself in it. The more I became a leading voice in the room, the more I realized how much I enjoyed it, how impactful it could be to stand in front of a crowd, and with nothing but words, change minds and beliefs, and perhaps even history. It helped, I am sure, that even as a teenager, I was blessed with an unusually deep baritone voice, one that lent my words the aura of authority, even when it hadn't been earned.

During my second summer at Ben-Shemen, the youth movement I had chosen to join—HaNoar HaOved, or Working Youth—voted to elect me as a delegate to its national convention. I was elated. I was no less committed to my dreams of settling the land, but I was suddenly aware that I had a skill others thought powerful—the ability to persuade. I felt I had been called to service, that circumstance was conspiring to create a second path for me.

A few months after accepting the position, I was required to make a trip up north to Haifa on behalf of HaNoar HaOved. I had planned to take a bus, but when I mentioned this plan to Berl Katznelson, an instructor and great Zionist thinker who had taken a liking to me, he suggested a better idea.

"Actually, the timing is perfect," he said. "I have a friend who is driving up to Haifa next week. I'm sure I can arrange to get you a seat in his car."

"That's excellent news," I said. "Who's your friend?"

"It's David Ben-Gurion," he replied nonchalantly.

In my mind, David Ben-Gurion was not just a man, but a legend. He was the leader of the Jewish people in Mandatory Palestine, part strategist, part philosopher. He sought independence for the Jews not only to create a state, but to fulfill our historic mission, to become a "light unto nations," an example for all of humanity. His vision for our future state—safe, secure, democratic, and socialist—was an inspiration to me, and the urgency with which he fought was a subject of constant admiration. Suddenly, I was going to get two hours with him, with nothing to interrupt us but time.

I slept very little the night before the journey. Instead, I spent most of the early hours of the morning considering what he might say to me, and how I might respond. I tried to imagine the questions he would ask, and tried to practice my answers, whispering quietly to myself as I stared at the ceiling. I couldn't help but think that if I could impress him, if I could show him my grasp of the issues and my commitment to the cause, then perhaps he would remember me—that maybe I could stand out. Who knew where that might lead?

I was sitting in the backseat when Ben-Gurion got into the car, and took the seat next to me. In person, his hair seemed even whiter than in photographs, almost glowing against the tanned skin of his mostly bald head. He was wearing an overcoat, and a frown on his face that seemed more reflective of the permanent position of his mouth than his disposition—or, at least, so I hoped.

As we pulled away he looked over at me and gave a small nod to acknowledge my presence. But before I could introduce myself, he had already turned away. He leaned his head against the window and closed his eyes, and within a few minutes, it became clear he was sleeping. There was no end to my disappointment.

He stayed asleep for nearly the entire journey. But as we got close to Haifa, the bouncing of car on the dirt road must have woken him. Through the corner of my eye, I could see him adjusting himself, wiping his eyes and fixing his posture. It seemed I might have my chance after all. Then without warning, he turned and shouted at me, "You know, Trotsky was no leader!"

I didn't know what to think—or what to say. I didn't understand how we landed on the topic, or why he seemed to think I was curious about Trotsky, or what it was he was even referring to. But how could I not be curious?

"Why do you say that?" I asked.

In 1918, following the Russian Revolution, Leon Trotsky had become the Soviet Union's first minister of foreign affairs. He had come to lead the Soviet delegation in peace negotiations to end Soviet Russia's involvement in World War I. Having grown impatient with Germany for demanding more and more territorial concessions, Trotsky decided to cut off negotiations altogether. Instead, he unilaterally declared an end of hostilities without signing an agreement with the Germans. Trotsky had described the proposal as "no war, no peace."

"'No war, no peace'?" Ben-Gurion shouted, his face red with anger. "What is this? This is not a strategy. This is an invention. Either peace and pay the price or war and take the risk—there is no other choice."

Again I was not sure how to respond, but this time it didn't matter. Before I could formulate a careful reply, Ben-Gurion had closed his eyes and returned to his nap. He didn't say another word.

. . .

After graduating from Ben-Shemen in 1941, a group of us were sent to Kibbutz Geva in the Jezreel Valley for further training. At Ben-Shemen, we had learned the skills we would need to cultivate the land. At Geva, we were to learn what it took to succeed on a kibbutz. I had two jobs. My first involved working the cornfields. Only when I was finished—usually after sundown—would I turn to my next job, as a coordinator of HaNoar HaOved movement across the Jordan and Jezreel Valleys. I was given a large and unwieldy Triumph motorcycle to use so I could meet with members from other chapters. We would hold meetings and debates, organize seminars and public discussions, and dedicate what was left of our waking hours to convincing the others we were right.

At the heart of these discussions lay the issue of territory. In 1917, the British government, which controlled much of the Middle East, issued the Balfour Declaration, which endorsed the idea of a national home for the Jewish people in the land of Israel. But many feared our future state would be relegated to a sliver of territory, too small and unnourished to sustain the Jewish people. They believed that we should be uncompromising, calling for a return to our ancient borders—even if such a demand would never be met. I disagreed. Like Ben-Gurion, I believed the dominant moral consideration was the survival of the nation, rather than the size of the state that would house it. And I feared, as he did, that the greatest danger of all was to reach for a state and fail.

The debates raged on from kibbutz to kibbutz. In the meantime, my circle of friends set off on the mission we'd been training for—trekking twenty-five miles north of Geva to the peak of Mount Poriya, where we were to become members of Kibbutz Alumot.

From the moment we arrived, I was in awe. I could look out in every direction and see something extraordinary. At the base of Poriya was the sparkling Sea of Galilee in all its beauty, its far banks stretching well beyond the horizon. There were magnificent mountains to the west, painted purple in long brushstrokes. There were rows of young saplings, newly planted, that would one day grow into groves of olives and dates. From the right vantage point, I could watch the pale silver bands of the Jordan River snaking its way through the valley. To the north, I could see the towering Mount Hermon—and, unobstructed, it could see me. All at once I felt I was at the center of the world. For so long I had imagined a life like this, and now it was realized in front of me, a most elegant argument for the virtue of dreaming.

Once I was settled into Alumot, I was assigned a job that would give me my first true experience as a leader—not of men, but of sheep. Yet there were striking similarities: a shepherd, for example, may have authority over his flock, but that alone does not mean he can control it. There were many times when I would lead the herd down the hill, intent on having them follow me, only to find them scattering across the fields, paying no mind to my commands. It took time and patience to master the skill. We had to find a common language, a common understanding. I had to know their fears as if they were my own, so I could understand where they could not be led—or at least, when I'd have to move with more deliberateness. I had to be both empathetic and insistent in stating my intentions—a figure they would follow, even reluctantly, if only out of trust.

On the good days, it was a beautiful dance, its own piece of poetry and a lesson in leadership that I'd long remember. But hard days, though less frequent, proved unavoidable facts of nature—these were beasts, not men—that could not be cured with sharpened skills. At my best, I could still experience the worst, and that was a lesson I took with me, too—in patience if nothing else.

Life at Alumot was not easy. Because of its location, the winds traveling through the valley would gain lift and power as they approached our settlement, tearing through the barns with incredible violence. The soil beneath our feet was saturated with salts that choked off our crops and, for the first several years, forced us to heavily ration our harvests. And for a time, the few members of Alumot resided in a cluster of sinister black basalt ruins of a previous settlement, one that had failed catastrophically twenty years earlier. It was as though we were living among tombstones, constant reminders that our efforts could fail.

It would have been easy for an outsider to measure Kibbutz Alumot by what it lacked. We lived in tents. There was no electricity or running water. Each person was given one pair of work boots, two pairs of khaki pants, and two shirts—one for work and one for the Sabbath. The kibbutz owned one pair of gray trousers and one British Army–issue battle-dress jacket, which were lent out to the men only on the most special of occasions. And yet those of us who lived there measured Kibbutz Alumot by what it offered. It gave us a sense of meaning and mission. It gave us a family larger than any we had known and a purpose that was greater than ourselves. The hardness wasn't an inconvenience; it was the reason we were there.

And so we worked. We cleared the rocks and rehabilitated the soil. We cut tracts through barren lands and sowed them with seeds until they had no choice but to yield to our efforts.

Each morning, long before dawn, I would open the pen for the sheep so they could head down the hill of Poriya and graze between rocks on the intermittent pastures. The path down was dangerously steep, even more so in the darkness. But by sunrise, the flies would return to torment the sheep, so it was better to feed them at night.

I didn't mind. If anything, I preferred the time alone. How many nights did I sit on a rock, watching the stars reflect in the stillness of the water below? Too many to count. In those days I wanted nothing more than to be a poet or an architect, to build something either from words or from stones. And what better place, I wondered, what greater perch in the world, for an aspiring writer to let his poetry take flight?

These were some of the happiest days of my life, and they were made all the more meaningful when Sonia chose to become part of them again. At the beginning of World War II, Sonia had enlisted in the British Army as a nurse, and had been stationed in Egypt. Now, having returned, she had decided to join me at Alumot. We were married under a simple white chuppah on Lag BaOmer, May 1, 1945, in a small ceremony at Ben-Shemen. I had to borrow Alumot's formal pants and jacket, which were a bit too short for me; I spent the eve of our wedding using shoe polish to dye the jacket black.

Then one morning, Ben-Gurion's closest advisor, Levi Eshkol, arrived at Alumot from his neighboring kibbutz, with a request from Ben-Gurion himself. Eshkol, the future prime minister, was already a giant in the movement in those days, someone whom we greatly admired, and it was a genuine shock to see him among us—even more so to learn he had come, in part, because of me. Ben-Gurion had grown worried that the youngest generation was drifting too far from his vision for a state of Israel. He believed the fate of the Jewish people rested in his winning the argument. This was why he had sent Eshkol: to request that Alumot release me from my agricultural obligations, turning my evening work with HaNoar HaOved into a full-time job. Ben-Gurion knew the young generation represented the future, and he must have felt they were more likely to be persuaded by one of their peers. At least that's what I told myself as I struggled to comprehend how it was possible that, of all people, Ben-Gurion had chosen me, in all my inexperience, to participate in such an important mission.

The moment I arrived at HaNoar HaOved headquarters in Tel Aviv, I understood exactly why Eshkol had come to find me. There were twelve members of HaNoar HaOveds secretariat, and it appeared that I was the only member who favored Ben-Gurion's approach to statehood. The meetings were so one-sided as to be totally useless. I was viewed with suspicion, seen only as Eshkol's mouthpiece. Any proposal I submitted was voted down immediately. Any argument I started was invariably silenced. It wasn't long before I decided that the only way to help the cause was to change the makeup of the secretariat itself. This would be possible only at HaNoar HaOved's national convention, and it would require the support of a majority of delegates in the room. Who those delegates would be—and whom they would ultimately support—was still an open question. And so rather than be swatted down day in and day out, I stopped going to Tel Aviv headquarters altogether and focused my efforts out in the field.

Again and again I drove the same roads on the same wily motorcycle, meeting with every chapter of HaNoar HaOved that would have me. At each stop I would advocate my own political views, pressing the urgency of Jewish statehood on behalf of all who could no longer afford to wait. I met with hundreds of people, making my case to anyone who would listen. I told them to make sure the delegates they sent to the convention were Ben-Gurionites, and asked them to vote against the secretariat and instead stand with me.

On September 28, 1945, the national convention of HaNoar HaOved was called to order at the Mugrabi Cinema in Tel Aviv. I was deeply nervous. In addition to the delegates in the hall, there were many prominent leaders of Ben-Gurion's political party, Mifleget Poalei Eretz Yisrael, which meant "Workers' Party of the Land of Israel," known colloquially as the Mapai. As delegates flooded into the hall, I stood at the registration desk, preparing a detailed list of who was attending and how they intended to vote. But I still wasn't certain of the outcome.

One of the first orders of business was the adoption of the platform. The delegates were given two choices. The first came from Binyamin Chochlovkin, the secretary-general of HaNoar HaOved, and represented the "Greater Israel" position. The alternative proposal was my own, and reflected the Mapai positon. Binyamin had the backing of the secretariat and the majority of the Zionist movement. But to his surprise, and frankly, to mine, I had the backing of the room. The delegates had determined that a partitioned Palestine today was clearly preferable to a "Greater Israel" tomorrow; when their votes were cast, my proposal carried the day.

Neither side had expected the outcome, which was made obvious by the ensuing chaos in the hall. I was greeted as a conquering victor by the Mapai leaders. By the end of the convention I was a leader in the movement, having been elected HaNoar HaOved's secretary-general. Suddenly my greatest heroes knew my name. I was no longer the anonymous boy sharing a car ride to Haifa.

• • •

On October 20, 1946, we had our first child, Tsvia, a beautiful bundle, whom we named after my beloved late maternal grandfather. We moved out of a tent and into a small house.

Later that year, the Twenty-Second Zionist Congress was to be held in Basel, Switzerland, the first such meeting since the Holocaust. The Twenty-First Congress, which had been held only days before the start of World War II, was adjourned with the foreboding words of Chaim Weizmann, president of the Zionist Organization and future first president of Israel: "I have no prayer but this: that we will all meet again alive."

The world had changed irrevocably even before the start of the war. In May 1939, the British government issued the "White Paper," a policy document that contained an incomprehensible betrayal of the Jewish people. It was a repudiation of the Balfour Declaration of 1917 by the United Kingdom's foreign secretary, which had favored "the establishment in Palestine of a national home for the Jewish people." Having decided that if the Jews were to live in Mandatory Palestine, they were to do so as a permanent minority, the British government now put stringent restrictions on Jewish immigration and froze our ability to continue to purchase land to settle. It was intended to be a death sentence for the Jewish state. And by preventing immigration it would also be a death sentence to countless Jews fleeing the grip of the Nazis. If we wanted our independence, we'd have to take on the British.

In September 1939, Hitler invaded Poland and began his quest for world domination and Jewish annihilation. Two days later, the British declared war against Germany, becoming, paradoxically, both our most important friend and our second-greatest enemy. Ben-Gurion had crystallized the complexity of the relationship, and the new Zionist challenge, this way: "We must help the British army as if there were no White Paper, and we must fight the White Paper as if there were no war."

And yet, despite the forces arrayed against the Jewish people, there were many on the left who had opposed Ben-Gurion's change in posture. They preferred the slow and steady progression of compromise to Ben-Gurion's more aggressive approach against the British. This infuriated Ben-Gurion, who saw no justification for inaction, certainly not in the midst of an attempted extinction.

By 1946, the war was over, and it had been time again to reconvene in Basel. The Mapai decided to send two of their younger members as part of their broader delegation, and I soon learned that Ben-Gurion had chosen me to be one of them. The other young man was a bit older than me, handsome, brilliant, and every bit as committed to Ben-Gurion as I was. His name was Moshe Dayan.

We boarded a ship together in December 1946, my first trip abroad since arriving in Jaffa more than a decade before. It seemed as though every member of the Zionist leadership was aboard, and somehow, here I stood among them.

On the upper deck, Moshe and I spent a great deal of time together. We were the youngest two on the vessel, and though we were vastly different from each other, we found an immediate friendship and mutual respect.

We spent hours engrossed in conversation about our views of the debate and our expectations for the conference. We both firmly believed in Ben-Gurion's position, willing to use force to support the unfettered continuation of immigration to Mandatory Palestine, whether the British deemed it illegal or not. At one point, Dayan had even suggested we burn down the camps where the British were detaining Jews who had been captured on the way to their homeland. Part strategist and part fighter, Dayan was both an equal and a mentor, a man I deeply admired.

There was something incredibly moving about entering the hall where the Congress was held. Nearly fifty years earlier, this was the same place that Theodor Herzl had convened the First Zionist Congress. History was alive in the room, and an uncertain future at stake for us all. From my seat I could see Weizmann, Eshkol, and Ben-Gurion on the dais, along with every other major figure in the Zionist movement.

I could also see the visibly empty chairs of those for whom Weizmann's 1939 prayer had not been answered. In his memoir, he wrote about the "dreadful experience" of presiding over the meeting, of standing before the assembly and "finding among them hardly one of the friendly faces which had adorned past Congresses." The largest delegations had come from Mandatory Palestine and the United States; with few exceptions, the room was eerily absent of European Jews.

And yet, despite the many thousands of Holocaust survivors who were being denied entry to Mandatory Palestine by the British, the conference had proceeded as though there were no real urgency. There was genuine debate about whether we should do what it took—whatever it took—to get the survivors to their homeland. Ben-Gurion was furious, understandably so—at the tepidity of politics; at the conference's obsession with the minutiae of bureaucracy; and most of all, at the lack of courage and commitment he knew we required. By the end of the first session, it had become clear that a deeply frustrated Ben-Gurion lacked support for his proposals.

I didn't see him the next morning, when the conference reconvened. I remember I was seated next to Arye Bahir, a leading voice in the Mapai party and a friend of Ben-Gurion. We were discussing our frustrations with what had transpired when suddenly Ben-Gurion's wife, Paula, entered the hall with a dark look on her face, walking as swiftly as she could directly toward us. She came right up to Bahir and leaned in closely, whispering to him in frantic Yiddish.

"Arye, he has gone mad," I heard her say. "You have to stop him," she insisted. "He's going to leave."

Though Bahir and I shared Ben-Gurion's frustrations with the conference, we both instinctively knew that his leaving would present a grave problem. He was viewed, even by his most vehement critics, as a uniquely resilient and visionary leader, the kind the movement could not succeed without. And he was surely the only one who could convince his fellow party members to support his plan for our future statehood. Paula was keenly aware of this. We hadn't been summoned to calm an argument; we'd been summoned to save the movement.

Bahir stood up with Paula, then signaled for me to join him. We left the hall and went up to the hotel room where Ben-Gurion was staying—the same room Herzl had occupied during the First Congress, in 1897. When we got to his door, we knocked several times, but there was no response. From somewhere inside me, I found the chutzpah to turn the knob. The door was unlocked. There he was, standing with his back to us, angrily shoving his clothing into an open suitcase.

"Shalom, Ben-Gurion," Bahir said tentatively. There was no answer. "Shalom?" Again no answer—no acknowledgment at all that we were there. Finally, Ben-Gurion spoke.

"Are you coming with me?" he asked.

"Where are you going?" Bahir asked.

"To form a new Zionist movement," he bellowed. "I have no more confidence in this Congress. It's full of small-time politicians, pathetic defeatists. They won't have the courage to make the decisions that are needed now.

"A third of our nation has been wiped out," he continued. "The survivors have no hope other than to rebuild their lives in our homeland. It's the only land that must open its gates wide to welcome them. Do they not see this?"

Then he looked briefly toward me, a wide-eyed twenty-three-year-old boy. "Only the Jewish youth will provide the courage needed to face this challenge."

Bahir told Ben-Gurion that of course we were with him, that wherever he went, we would go, that there was no hope for Zionism without him. Once Ben-Gurion realized that we were true allies, he calmed down enough that we could have an extended conversation. What we had told him was true: he had become the center of gravity for the movement—the one leader we could not live without. But we also knew that his walking away to start a new movement was not a solution to the problem of urgency. It would surely take years to organize such an effort, years we simply did not have to spare. And so Bahir and I suggested the only option we could think of. Before walking away from the Congress, we wanted Ben-Gurion to try to convince the Mapai faction one last time of his vision. "If there's a majority there, we'll all stay; and if not, we won't be the only ones to leave with you; a great many more will come, too." After much consideration, and some serious reservation, Ben-Gurion finally agreed.

It didn't take long before word spread among the Mapai about Ben-Gurion's anger and intentions. Bahir and I weren't the only ones who understood the stakes of losing Ben-Gurion in the fight. That evening, they convened a meeting of the Mapai, chaired by Golda Meir. Golda was already a giant in the Zionist cause, and a close friend and advisor to Ben-Gurion. She would later become one of only two women to sign Israel's declaration of independence, as well as its fourth prime minister. The debate was a brutal back-and-forth of arguments and emotions that went straight through the night. The final vote was called as the sun was coming up. When Golda was finished counting, we learned the result: Ben-Gurion had won with a razor-thin majority. The activist approach had prevailed. The movement remained alive.

It was a tremendously important victory, and not just on the immediate policy front. It felt to me and many others as though Ben-Gurion was unstoppable, that nothing and no one could prevent us from achieving our mission. Indeed, in that moment I felt as though the Jewish state had just been born, along with something new and powerful inside me. For the first time, I admitted to myself that a life of poetry and shepherding was not enough to contain my dreams. I had wanted so badly to join the pioneers. But to fight for a Jewish state in that way Ben-Gurion had just done— with urgent, imaginative, and moral leadership—this, too, was a frontier, and it was calling me to service.

Returning home to Sonia and Tsvia, it was impossible not to look back with enormous admiration at Ben-Gurion's triumph. Of course, he had won the debate as a result of his brilliant rhetoric and, I firmly believed, the rightness of his claims. But I had seen something else, too, something that would strongly influence my thinking about leadership: when he had been most frustrated, most intent on walking away, he had remained open to the arguments made by two young men with a mere fraction of his experience and wisdom. He had nearly given up on the larger debate, but he had not given up on his belief *in* debate. During my career, I would encounter numerous situations in which parties found themselves full of mistrust and anger, where it seemed that all doors had been closed. Ben-Gurion had shown me that listening is not just a key element of good leadership, it is *the* key, the means to unlock doors that have been slammed shut by bitter dispute and resignation.

Little did I know how often I would end up thinking back to that moment in the hotel room—or how soon.

CHAPTER 2

INDEPENDENCE, ALLIANCE, AND THE FIGHT FOR SECURITY

On a bright and beautiful afternoon in May 1947, I sat in a chair at the edge of the mountainside, nursing two goats. A great band of fog was collecting below on the banks of the Kinneret, infusing the wind with a delicate mist.

"Shimon? Shimon!" I heard from behind. I turned to see a close friend running frantically toward me.

I stood up, surprised, concerned. "What is it?" I asked.

"Levi Eshkol is here again," he said through panted breaths. "He's here with a letter from Ben-Gurion."

"What is it about?"

He paused again to catch his breath.

"You," he stammered. "It's about you."

Eshkol, I would soon learn, was there to retrieve me. All the members of the kibbutz were called to a special meeting, where the contents of the letter were shared. He was writing to ask that I once again be relieved of my important kibbutz duties so that I could undertake another effort, allowing me to serve the underground Jewish army, known as the Haganah—which would later become the Israel Defense Forces (IDF). Though it was Ben-Gurion making the request, the rules dictated that Alumot's members would have to vote to release me. And so Ben-Gurion aimed not to command, but to persuade. He was convinced that our War of Independence was coming, which meant that military preparedness and a focus on security would become our next great imperative. "Look at this as one of the many tasks of the kibbutz, a new field to work," he wrote, hoping to convince the kibbutz membership that this new mission was central to their own. After a brief deliberation, and in common cause, the members voted to honor Ben-Gurion's wishes. I was to report to Haganah headquarters, an unassuming red house (known, uncreatively, as "The Red House") on HaYarkon Street in Tel Aviv.

It was a call I was proud to answer, but how I could help, I wasn't quite sure. I had no training beyond defending Ben-Shemen. I knew nothing of building armies or preparing for war.

When I walked into the Red House, I was relieved to see a person I recognized, a fellow member of Kibbutz Alumot. "Do you know where I'm supposed to go?" I asked.

"No," he said. "No one told me you were coming. Do you know what you're supposed to be doing?"

"No, I don't know. Ben-Gurion sent for me."

"I see. Well, Yaakov Dori, the chief of staff, is quite ill, so his desk and chair are empty. Why don't you sit there for now?"

A few hours later, Ben-Gurion entered the offices, flanked

on either side by military advisors. As he walked by, he caught a glimpse of me from the corner of his eye.

"Shimon, good, you're here," he said, fishing from his pocket a few sheets of well-worn paper, which he handed to me. It was a list in two columns, one short and one long.

"These are the weapons we have," he said, pointing to the first column, "and these are the weapons we need. If we shall have only what we have, we are finished."

Ben-Gurion's concerns were not without merit. Developments in the United Nations suggested that the General Assembly was likely to vote on a resolution that would create a partitioned Palestine, and lead to the establishment of a Jewish state. In isolation, this was cause for elation. But Ben-Gurion was deeply worried. He expected that war would be declared on the newly formed Jewish state, both from inside its new borders and from its Arab neighbors. What good is the birth of a new state, he would say, if it's immediately strangled in its crib? Ben-Gurion set out to transform the Haganah for this very reason: to ensure that the newly formed state wouldn't find itself without a military to defend itself. "This will no longer be a war of platoons," he said. "It is essential to set up a modern army."

"What can I do?" I asked Ben-Gurion as he handed me the extensive shopping list of weapons.

"It's simple," he said. "Find these weapons for us as fast as you can."

I returned to my borrowed desk to review the document, but found it was like reading a shopping list in a language I didn't speak. I opened the desk drawer to get a notepad and pencil to start taking notes when I noticed, inside the desk, a letter addressed to

Ben-Gurion that Dori must have saved. It was written by one of our generals, one who had been offered the position of chief of staff and, as the letter indicated, had chosen to turn it down.

"I don't desire to be chief of staff for six days," he wrote, an explanation that made little sense to me until I asked a colleague to explain it.

"Why did the general turn down the job?" I asked.

"A lot of reasons."

"Like what?"

"The bullets," he said.

"What do you mean?"

"Look at the list," he said, pointing at one of the entries for what we already had. "Six million bullets."

"That sounds like a lot," I admitted. The man laughed.

"When the war comes, we'll need a million bullets a day." Before walking away, he added, "Not an easy job."

This was what the general had meant—that he was not willing to wage a defensive war with less than a week's worth of ammunition. It was stunning to hear for two reasons: First, I knew—all of us knew—that the state would face danger in war. Great danger, even. But grave danger? To be so ill-equipped that we would exhaust our supply of ammunition before week's end was a terrifying prospect. But even more shocking than the revelation itself was the notion that someone so expert could be asked to assist in such an important cause and would turn it down because it seemed too hard. Ben-Gurion was not asking for help on a side project with little importance; he was asking the general to help with the most central project of all: the defense of a state not yet born, and the realization of the Zionist dream. The magnitude of the challenge may have seemed overwhelming, but what possible answer was worthy of our history—and our future—other than an emphatic and hopeful "yes"?

I could hear my grandfather's words echoing in my mind: "Always remain Jewish." Being Jewish meant many things to me, but first and foremost it meant having the moral courage to do what was required on behalf of the Jewish people. At the time, I may have lacked the experience and rank to know much about the weapons on Ben-Gurion's list, but decisions needed to be made about ammunition and alliances and weapons and war, and rather than run from the challenge, I fully embraced it.

. . .

I am perceived by many to be a man of great contradictions. For the past forty years I have been known as one of Israel's most vocal doves, as a man singularly focused on peace. But the first two decades of my career were spent not in pursuit of peace but in preparation for war. For a time, it was said that I was one of Israel's most assertive hawks. In this it is assumed that I must have changed, that my efforts and outlook were defined by a sweeping moral transformation. There is a certain poetry to that narrative, but it invents a paradox where none actually exists. It was not me that changed; it was the situation that changed.

Peace is a purpose—a goal worthy of the chase, while war is a function—born out of reluctant necessity. No rational person could prefer the latter. When peace first appeared possible, I pursued it with all of my energies. When Arab leaders were open to negotiation, I said I prefer negotiation, too. The vision of the prophets was one of peace and justice, of morality and tolerance. "And they shall beat their swords into plowshares, and their spears into pruning hooks," the Torah tells us. "Nation shall not lift up sword against nation, neither shall they learn war anymore." This was the guiding vision of the Jewish people. But it must be remembered that there was a time when our circumstances were quite different; a time when, rather than negotiate, our Arab neighbors sought only to destroy us. There was a time when Israel stood defenseless in a sea of enemies, a time of extraordinary and constant danger. These were the years before peace was possible—the years when I was a hawk without compromise.

Our neighbors' malign intentions were not the only reason we faced almost certain destruction. The Middle East was under a Western arms embargo, as the United States, the British, and the French pledged to remain neutral in its affairs. In practice, Israel was the only real victim of the embargo; the Soviets were eagerly supplying weapons to the Arab states that were threatening our destruction, even if the West was not supplying us. Thus, our enemies had a free flow of weapons to equip their already vast armies, while we had six days' worth of ammunition, a militia made up largely of farmers and Holocaust survivors with no formal training—and no clear path to the weapons we would depend upon once attacked.

The only way to protect ourselves was to break the embargo—to purchase weapons illegally, and secretly bring them home.

Days earlier, I had been milking cows on a kibbutz. Now I was being thrown into one of the most dramatic periods of my life. I would build friendships with arms dealers and partnerships with arms smugglers. I would undertake secret missions using fake passports, working in the shadows to purchase as much as I could. In time, I developed an expertise, both in granular details of the arms we were seeking, and in the work it would take to acquire them. I would learn everything from the defects inherent in a particular type of rifle, to the fuel supply needed to carry a warship across the Atlantic. And I would become well versed in the strange combination of deference and demand that was required to get the best equipment delivered on time. But at the beginning, all I knew was that my task was essential and there was no time to waste. I was intensely curious to learn all I could about these technical details, but I was not at all curious about the reason I had to do so: it went without thinking.

There was only one country that was willing to send us arms directly: Czechoslovakia. The other satellite nations behind the Iron Curtain had joined the arms boycott against us, but Stalin saw opportunity in the Western embargo, believing that a show of support might bring our young socialist country closer to his communist empire. And so he let the Czechs supply us with the arms we desperately needed. There was a stunning symbolism to what we received; most had been manufactured at facilities set up by the Nazis in occupied Czech territory. The very same weapons that had once been used against us would now be used to try to protect us.

Within six months of my having arrived at the Haganah headquarters, I had helped stockpile an incredible trove of arms—and just in time. During the last week of November 1947, the United Nations General Assembly's two-month-long debate on UN Resolution 181 came to a head. If the resolution were adopted, it would put an end to the British mandate and partition Palestine into two states, one Arab and one Jewish, thereby leading to our declaration of independence, and likely to armed conflict. But none of us knew, inside or outside government, if the resolution had the votes to prevail. Its adoption required a two-thirds majority of member nations, a challenge more akin to scaling a cliff than climbing a mountain. On November 26, we listened to the debate on our radios, as the representatives of nation after nation came to speak, holding our destiny in their hands.

The Arab nations were uniformly opposed to the resolution, making the case that the UN lacked the authority to even consider the matter. The representative from Saudi Arabia referred to the resolution as a "flagrant aggression," and was followed by the Syrian representative, who called it "the greatest political scandal of all time." The USSR, which had once opposed the partition plan, was the first to support the resolution, arguing that the one-state solution was "unworkable and impractical." In the same speech, the representative dismissed the claims of the Arab nations, insisting that the UN not only had the right to intervene in the name of international peace, but was duty-bound by its charter to do so.

When the debate was over, it remained unclear whether we had enough support. Even on the day of the vote—November 29, 1947—there were still seven nations that hadn't announced their intentions. And though we had gotten commitments from a great many nations, we weren't convinced that all would be kept.

As dusk settled over Tel Aviv, scores of people gathered in Magen David Square, where loudspeakers had been set up to broadcast the vote. As the static cleared, we could hear Osvaldo Aranha, the president of the General Assembly, call for a vote on the resolution. We listened attentively, along with Jewish communities from all over the world.

"Afghanistan? No. Argentina? Abstention. Australia? Yes."

Every nation called, every answer called back, rang in our ears until it felt we had stopped breathing entirely. Ben-Gurion and I paced as we listened, as though our steps had the power to speed up time.

"El Salvador? Abstention. Ethiopia? Abstain. France? Yes." At this there was a sudden commotion in the hall, followed by an aggressive banging of the gavel.

"I call on the public, and I hope that you will not have any interference on the voting in this debate," the president of the General Assembly warned, apparently addressing the gathered crowd in the gallery. "I am confident in the way you will behave regarding this serious decision taken by this assembly," he continued sternly, "because I have decided not to allow anybody to interfere in our decision!"

The moments passed. People held tight to each other in the square as the remaining votes were cast, hoping, if not yet believing, that something extraordinary was about to happen.

"Uruguay? Yes. Venezuela? Yes? Yemen? No. Yugoslavia? Abstain." Again we heard the gavel bang, this time to signify the end of voting. And then, the simple words that would change the course of Jewish history: "The resolution . . . was adopted by thirty-three votes; thirteen against, ten abstentions."

A raucous cheer exploded from the crowd. There were warm embraces and incredulous laughter, tears of hope and of joy, moments of reflection. As word traveled through Tel Aviv, Jews took to the streets in a spontaneous outpouring. Ben-Gurion and I stood together as we watched thousands of Jews joining hands with one another, dancing the hora over and over again. Never once, in our two thousand years of exile, had there been a more ambitious dream for our people than the dream to return home. It had been just over fifty years since Theodor Herzl started the movement "to lay the foundation stone of the house which is to shelter the Jewish Nation." By the standards of world history, we had achieved this with remarkable speed. But by the standards of our recent history, most immediately the murder of six million innocents and near extinction of European Jewry, we could never forget that we were nearly too late.

It was easy to get swept up in the wonder of the moment, but Ben-Gurion and I knew the celebration was premature. A United Nations resolution alone would not guarantee us our state.

"Today they are dancing in the street," he said to me with a wariness in his voice. "Tomorrow, they will have to shed blood in the street."

He was right. In the days after the resolution, we began to get reports of Arab militiamen attacking Jews in the settlements. We received harrowing cables from around the Middle East, of Jews being attacked in retaliation for the vote. There were detailed accounts of devastation—of synagogues and homes turned to ash in Syria, of mobs chasing down Jews from Egypt to Lebanon. The Arab League had declared its intentions—to prevent the resolution from being enacted and force the Jews out—to destroy the State of Israel before it could ever be drawn on a map. They had begun the process of carrying through on that dark pledge.

It was in that context that Ben-Gurion put in motion an effort to draft a formal declaration of independence. Though the British lost their mandate in the region as soon as the United Nations resolution had passed in November, a firm date had not been set for them to leave. Now it appeared that they would pull their final troops out of Israel on Friday night, May 14, 1948, at the stroke of midnight. Ben-Gurion intended to make his declaration just prior to their departure, to ensure no gap between the end of the British mandate and the beginning of our independence.

During the rare quiet moments in those otherwise frenetic days, it wasn't only the work ahead that occupied my thoughts; it was my firstborn daughter, Tsvia, who knew nothing of the world but the love of her parents. Tsvia, who had just learned how to call for her father. *"Abba, Abba!"* I could hear her say over and over in my mind—a beautiful if haunting reminder of what was at stake in the battle to come.

On the afternoon of May 14, 1948, in the final hours before the Sabbath, I sat at my desk preparing for war, while Ben-Gurion stood at the center of a dais in the Tel Aviv Museum of Art, prepared to say the words that would consecrate our state. Because of the extraordinary security risks, we ensured that the guests and journalists present had only learned of the meeting and its location in the minutes before it began. As ministers made their way past the honor guard of the Haganah and through the flashbulbs of photographers, the commotion attracted cheering crowds to the streets. The attendees entered one of the museum's galleries to the sound of the soon to be named Israel Philharmonic Orchestra playing. The walls were filled with works from the private collection of Tel Aviv's mayor—Meir Dizengoff—paintings by Jewish artists that depicted Jewish life during two millennia in exile.

The thirteen temporary governing ministers took their place on the dais, on either side of Ben-Gurion. Behind the man who had led the Jewish people to this moment was a portrait of the man who started us on our journey: Herzl was now watching over the culmination of a dream he had for us all.

Ben-Gurion gaveled the room to order and, wildly enthusiastic, those assembled broke out in a spontaneous rendition of "Hatikvah," the Zionist anthem that had been banned by the British. Then Ben-Gurion said the words that all who gathered had waited a lifetime to hear: "We hereby proclaim the establishment of the Jewish state in Palestine, to be called Israel." The room erupted with a combination of the boisterous applause of victory, and the gentle tears of grief. It was, at once, a reminder of how far we'd come, and of how much we had lost.

At the end of the ceremony, the orchestra played "Hatikvah" while the audience stood in respectful silence. What they had sung together earlier was a call to action for a nation, dispersed but with a common dream. Now it was so much more—not just a rallying cry of hope, but a melody of historic vindication; not just the anthem of a movement, but the anthem of a sovereign state.

Israel's public radio station broadcast the event live. The declaration traveled with tremendous speed across the country and around the world. In their modest homes, in the midst of great uncertainty, the people of Israel heard Ben-Gurion's words. They listened on behalf of the millions who had perished at the hands of the Nazis, and the millions more who remained in constant danger around the world. They listened on behalf of the past—on behalf of the pioneers who first set out on a journey toward home, who found imagination in necessity, and used it to carve a path. And they listened on behalf of the future, on behalf of generations of Jewish children and grandchildren not yet born, from whom our centuries-long fight drew its sole purpose.

Predictably, as soon as we had our independence, we faced war from all sides. On May 15, Syria, Egypt, Jordan, and Iraq attacked. In the north, Syria sent a brigade equipped with tanks and armored vehicles and an artillery battalion to attack the Jewish settlements on the other side of the Kinneret. The Egyptian military invaded from the south, assailing the nearby cities, settlements, and kibbutzim. They conducted bombing raids of Israeli airfields and southern settlements, and eventually of the central bus station in Tel Aviv, which they destroyed. Jordan, meanwhile, was marching its Arab Legion into Jerusalem, where it instigated some of the heaviest fighting of the war, in the process cutting off supplies and creating a dangerous shortage of food and water, not just for the soldiers but for the people of the city.

Outnumbered and outgunned, we refused to be outmatched, and our forces used whatever they had to defend their positions. At Kibbutz Degania, Syrian forces were stopped in their tracks by a resistance force of Israelis, equipped with Molotov cocktails and hand grenades. So it went in settlement after settlement, where Israelis fought back, repelling the advances of Arab forces. With the arrival of a major weapons shipment from Czechoslovakia, the Israeli Air Force was able to take to the sky and respond with powerful attacks, sending the advancing Egyptians into chaos and effectively ending the Iraqi incursion.

With the British no longer controlling the borders, a flood of Jewish immigrants made their way to Israel. Some had gone straight from Nazi concentration camps into refugee camps, where they had to wait permission to make their way to Israel. In Cyprus, for example, some twenty-two thousand Jews waited for two years. Others had been forced out of neighboring Arab nations more recently. They arrived without homes, after dangerous journeys, and turned right around to fight on behalf of their new state. We had started the war in May 1948 with fewer than thirty-five thousand troops. Before the end of the fighting in 1949, more than one hundred thousand had taken up arms for the Zionist cause.

The IDF battled on the front lines with extraordinary courage, following the orders of Ben-Gurion as he managed strategy from headquarters. War plans were defined and ordered there. Intelligence was processed and analyzed there. It was as if the heroes on the great lines were the beating heart of the effort while the headquarters was its brain. Without spare moments for deep contemplation and patient analysis, we were doing all that we could to shape the modern infrastructure of the military that our new state, under fire, was trying to assemble. At times rest seemed as distant a dream as victory.

The distance between Ben-Gurion's responsibilities and my own were vast by any measure. But the distance between our offices was, for a time, only the width of a thin piece of plywood. This made it possible for Ben-Gurion and me to build a relationship during those stressful months, one that eventually transformed me from one of his greatest admirers to one of his closest advisors.

Such a surprising turn of events I could not have imagined only months earlier. But the bonds formed during times of crisis are unusually strong. At first, our partnership developed quite informally. Ben-Gurion seemed to like how hard I could work, and how little sleep I tended to need or desire. (I even kept one of his handwritten notes on my desk, which read simply, "Shimon, don't forget to turn off the lights!") Over time, he began to trust me and to rely on me, in ways that surprised those who were more experienced and senior than I.

"Why do you trust that boy?" I would overhear them asking. His answer was always the same.

"Three reasons," he would say. "He doesn't lie. He doesn't say bad things about other people. And when he knocks on my door, he usually has a new idea." It was too simple an answer to persuade my detractors, but for me, it was the perfect response to a question I had so often asked of myself: Why me? In time, my relationship with Ben-Gurion would expand, both in personal trust and in formal responsibility, as I rose through the ranks of government. But for as long as Ben-Gurion lived, my formal position never reflected the scope of my influence or the depth of our bond.

By early 1949, the Arab nations were on the defensive—injured, in retreat, and exhausted from war. What Israel had lacked in resources we had made up for with ingenuity and organization. And what our enemies had bountifully possessed they thankfully had squandered in the chaos. In February, the Egyptians relented, signing an armistice agreement and giving up the fight. One month later, Lebanon signed, and in April, Jordan did the same. The last holdout—Syria—gave in on July 20, 1949. By then we had run through our weapons stockpiles, leaving us vulnerable and exposed. For the time, though, the war was over, replaced with an armistice we knew to be fragile and uneasy. For all that was lost—all the lives that were lost—there was to be no doubt of what was gained: control of our own territory and, indeed, our own destiny.

· · ·

During my first days at Haganah headquarters—before the War of Independence, before the United Nations resolution—I had an unusual encounter. I had been sitting at my desk reviewing documents when I heard a thundering commotion erupt from inside Levi Eshkol's office. Teddy Kollek, who at the time headed the Haganah's mission in the United States, had flown back to Tel Aviv for the very fight he was now engaged in. For months he had grown increasingly furious about the disorganization at headquarters. He had come to complain vigorously to Eshkol, citing, among other things, dozens of cables he'd sent to Tel Aviv that had gone ignored and unanswered. Our underground contacts in the United States had become one of our most important sources of arms, Kollek reminded Eshkol, and such disarray, he insisted, could be our undoing. Finally, Kollek gave Eshkol an ultimatum: assign someone to respond promptly to all of his cables, or accept his resignation.

I didn't know any of this when I heard Eshkol shouting my nickname through the door.

"Jungermann!" he yelled, Yiddish for "young man." *"Jungermann!"*

When I entered Eshkol's office, Kollek was still visibly angry.

"Oh good, here he is," Eshkol said in Hebrew. *"Jungermann,* do you know English?" he asked.

"No," I replied.

"Have you been to America?"

"No," I replied again.

Eshkol cracked the slightest smile. "Perfect," he said. "You're just the man I need."

Kollek was incredulous—and instantly enraged—but Eshkol paid him no attention.

"Don't worry," he replied coolly. "He'll do a better job than anyone."

With this, he excused me from his office and I returned to my desk, a bit embarrassed by the scene. Eventually, as the war went on, Kollek would learn that he could trust me, that I would respond to his cables with diligence and deliberateness. Nevertheless, the memory of that morning stayed with me like a pinched nerve in my spine, a prodding reminder of my own deficiencies.

And deficiencies there most certainly were. Without English, I lacked a common language with most of the world, and that, I knew, would hamper me. But English was just a small part of it. During the war, Ben-Gurion had come to rely on my advice, and I feared the well I'd been drawing from was insufficiently deep. I had been thrown into a world where knowledge of global affairs and of history was essential, where facility with economics and political science was the prerequisite of wisdom. I hadn't gone to university. I hadn't even earned a high school diploma. What talents I naturally possessed had been sufficient to this point, but it seemed inevitable that I would hit a ceiling; for all I knew, I already had.

In the spring of 1949, with our independence secured, I approached Ben-Gurion and explained my concerns, and asked his permission to rectify them. I told him that I wanted to go to New York to finish my education, and at the same time, represent Israel as part of the Defense Ministry's mission in America. With his enthusiastic blessing it was settled. On June 14, 1949, Sonia, Tsvia, and I made our way to the other side of the world.

Once in New York, we moved into a seven-room apartment on the Upper West Side of Manhattan, at the corner of Ninety-Fifth Street and Riverside Drive. We called our apartment "the kibbutz," because we shared it with several others, mostly men who worked for the Israeli government. Sonia would cook breakfast for everyone on Sundays, and each of our roommates took turns babysitting Tsvia. From our windows we could see bands of majestic elm trees, and behind them the glittering reflection of the sun on the Hudson River.

I enrolled in night classes at the New School for Social Research, which turned out to be a most remarkable institution. Its faculty included some of the world's most decorated intellectuals, people like Justice Felix Frankfurter, who could enchant the whole student body with his ambitious, if occasional, lectures. The New School would become one of the most formative places of my life, a source of learning I still depend on more than six decades later.

The early months were difficult. Taking courses that required a fluency in English at the same time that I was learning the language proved frustrating at times. But within a few months, I could comfortably engage someone in conversation. That's when the real New York became fully alive to me. I was taken by how highly people spoke of one another, how willing they were to give credit to others. I loved how generous they were with subtle acts of kindness. I loved, too, the myriad accents that punctuated the city—so many of us still learning to speak English. It seemed the ambitious promise of the United States was alive in the minds of all who had come there—as though the "American Dream" were its own force of nature.

I would often return to the "kibbutz" after class and continue reading my textbooks well into morning. Those hours alone were an enchanted intellectual ballet—but no matter how few hours that left for sleeping, I still arose every morning with a job to do.

Though the war was over, the posture of the American mission hadn't changed. Israel did not have the weapons to defend itself. Our stockpiles had been decimated by the war, leaving us with mismatched artillery and makeshift aircraft, our defensive chances almost entirely reliant on a team of engineers of robust will and expert repair skills. Yet the Western embargoes remained in place. Even the United States, whose early recognition of the state had been so generous, refused to sell us weapons at these most vulnerable early moments. We were left without choices at a time of unparalleled stakes. And so we took the only path forward, as I rejoined the strange world of black market dealings, and set about building a national defense force.

It seemed there were countless adventures. Once, I arranged to meet with arms dealers in Cuba at the Tropicana Hotel. They had set the meeting for twelve o'clock. But when I arrived at the hotel that afternoon and asked to be let in, the guard laughed in my face. Through his broken English, I realized what he thought was so funny: the meeting wasn't scheduled for noon; it was scheduled for midnight. What a novice I must have appeared to be. It was certainly an early lesson about the kind of work—and kind of people—I was dealing with. On another occasion, I arranged to purchase two British destroyers that the Colombian government no longer needed. I worked out the deal with the Colombian president and foreign minister in Bogotá, but before signing, I needed to fly to the port of Cartagena to inspect the ships myself. A senior Colombian general escorted me to a small airport, where we boarded a well-worn plane. About an hour into the flight, somewhere over the dense rain forest, the left engine of the plane burst into flames. The burly general looked to me with panic in his eyes.

"You have to decide what to do," he said.

"What are our options?" I asked him, trying to remain calm.

"We can crash-land in the jungle, but I think it could take us weeks to hike out."

"And the other option?"

"Keep flying to Cartagena and hope the plane doesn't explode."

I paused for a moment. "I'll take option two." We continued on our dangerous journey, each silenced by fear. Thankfully, the trip ended safely on a runway (and the destroyers were in excellent condition).

Still, for all the international excitement, most of our work was focused on deals we could broker in the United States. There we bought tanks and airplanes and all kinds of artillery, often from suspiciously sinister characters. We then had to smuggle them out of the country in parts, something made possible only by a partnership we had forged with the Teamsters, the labor union that represented the truckers. One of our most sympathetic and helpful advocates was the head of Detroit's local Teamsters chapter, a man named Jimmy Hoffa.

But of all the characters I worked with during those years, none was more fascinating, more boisterous, or more singularly invaluable to our efforts than a decorated Jewish-American pilot and aviation engineer named Al Schwimmer. During the War of Independence, Al joined the Israeli Air Force along with a raucous crew of fellow American pilots, where they quickly developed a reputation for being uncommonly brave, if a bit reckless and rowdy.

When the war was over, Al returned to California, but he remained deeply committed to the cause of our newborn state. On
a remote corner of a quiet airfield just north of Los Angeles, he
rented a modest airplane hangar—not much more than an over-
sized shed. He purchased a sparse collection of tools and hired a
small crew he knew he could trust, among them his fellow pilots
from our war. Inside the hangar, in what looked—at best—like
a makeshift operation conceived of by amateurs, Al and his team
had created, in secret, an impressively agile maintenance shop on
our behalf.

It seemed impossible, at first glance, that Al's team could build
the first aircraft for El Al, the newly created Israeli airline, whose
name means "to the skies." And yet this was the very thing they
intended to do. In retrospect, this is less surprising than it was
then. I have known a great many people of tremendous talent in
my life—but I don't know that I've ever known someone as good
at their craft as Al Schwimmer was at his. With a remarkable lack
of resources, he and his team seemed capable of fixing and flying
any plane in any circumstance. I remember a time when I had tried
and failed to purchase thirty surplus Mustang aircraft before the
U.S. military destroyed them (as was standard with such matériel).
Having escaped my grasp, the planes had been cut in two, and had
their wings amputated for good measure. But to Al's team, this
was merely a minor detail: they quickly purchased the parts from a
Texas junkyard, reassembled and tested the planes, then disassem-
bled them for shipment to Israel.

Over time this alliance with Al became one of our most important relationships. Whatever planes we purchased in the United
States we sent to Al. Sometimes he would fly the finished aircraft

to Israel himself, by way of the North Pole—not a particularly safe route, but easily the shortest. We concocted all sorts of schemes to smuggle the planes out of the United States, including a cover story that the planes were part of a movie. (Al actually set up a fictitious movie company, and I hired extras, to create the impression that the planes were taking off as part of a live-action scene. But rather than returning to the runway, they were flown directly to Czechoslovakia, where they were loaded with weaponry and ammunition, bound for Israel.)

During one of my visits to California, Al asked for my assistance with a rescue operation. One of our best pilots, Roy Kurtz, had gone down over Newfoundland while attempting to transport a plane to Israel. Al wanted to conduct a search-and-rescue operation, but to do so he needed quiet access to an Israeli aircraft. Given Al's risk-loving reputation, El Al had been reluctant to offer up one of their assets for such a dangerous mission. Eventually, I was able to secure their agreement, as long as I accepted their one condition: that I never leave the plane's sight.

For seven days we flew over the icy wasteland, making ever-larger concentric circles around where Al thought the crash might have occurred. At night, we would land on an airstrip in Goose Bay in Labrador, Canada, then return at daylight to the skies. Those hours aloft were tedious yet powerful. As we surveyed the land below, we fell into deep conversations that lasted for days— conversations about our highest aspirations and our deepest anxieties; conversations about Israel and its precarious position given the unsustainable nature of our current defenses.

After seven days, we had to face the tragic reality that Kurtz was not to be found. But I like to think that the mission was not in vain, that as a posthumous act of patriotism, Kurtz had brought Al and me together. As we searched for him over the tundra, Al and I arrived together at the same ambitious conclusion, one that had the power to transform Israeli security: to defend itself, Israel would need to be able to repair its own planes—and build new ones. We would need to take Al's California-based operation and move it to Israel, then invest in a massive expansion, transforming the enterprise from a wily start-up into a full-fledged aircraft industry. Doing so would extend the lives of the aircraft we were purchasing (wherever we were purchasing them from); in addition, Israel's hangars were filled with war-damaged albeit repairable aircraft—if only we'd had the facilities to make such repairs. There was also an opportunity for profit, Al argued: The world was still flooded with thousands of surplus World War II aircraft. Al believed he could buy them, repair them, and then export them to other countries—serving not just a military function but creating a commercial industry. We even fantasized about a time when we would be able to design and build our own planes.

It was a beautiful dream. I imagined a world where Al and his team were based in Tel Aviv, where his ingenuity could be leveraged without the limitations of distance. I imagined a world where each plane that we purchased could double or triple its flying life, allowing us to increase the size of our fleet many times over. It wouldn't solve all of our security challenges at once, but it could put us on course to solve many of them. The idea expanded in my mind like an aging star, with a great heat and grand brightness that displaced other thoughts. For the rest of our flights together, and in the days and weeks to come, I was preoccupied with tactical questions, eager to make real the world Al and I had together imagined.

An idea so bold would surely face headwinds. In the years after the War of Independence, Israel had plunged into financial crisis. We were recovering from a costly war at the same time that we were encouraging—and experiencing—a mass immigration. In three years we had doubled the population from six hundred thousand to 1.2 million, but we hadn't yet built a state that could sustain it. The new arrivals were forced to subsist in immigrant camps that were little more than tent cities. Food was provided by the government in communal dining halls, but it was strictly rationed. In some new immigrant camps, there was only one toilet for as many as fifty people. The conditions were harsh and unsanitary by any measure, and yet by 1952 more than 220,000 people were forced to live this way. Those who had settled in Israel early also faced intense rationing, instructed by the government about how much food they could purchase—even how many pairs of shoes they could own. Poverty was the central condition of our young state, a national emergency worthy of our urgent attention.

Given all this, what other response could I expect from my fellow Israelis except skepticism? I knew there would be those who dismissed the idea without a thought, considering it a preposterous notion from an idealistic young man. And yet I also knew that I was right, and that in being right, I should be willing to stand alone, that the doubts of those without imagination were no reason to abandon an important idea.

And so I made the decision to pursue the building of an aviation industry in a country without enough food for its people. Ben-Gurion had called upon me to help secure the state, and it was him, first and foremost, I hoped to convince. By stroke of luck, I learned that he would be making his first trip to America as prime minister and planned to include a stopover in California. To believe in Al's idea, Ben-Gurion would first have to believe in Al, and that, I knew, would only be achieved if he could see the possibility for himself.

When he arrived at Al's workshop, Ben-Gurion was astonished. Al and I escorted him through the hangar and demonstrated some of the team's best work. At one point, Al pointed out the equipment the team used to repair and rebuild the aircraft.

"What?" Ben-Gurion asked in utter surprise. "With this tiny collection of machines, you can renovate planes?"

Schwimmer nodded.

"We need something like this in Israel," Ben-Gurion replied. "Even more, we need a real aviation industry. We need to be independent." It was exactly what I had hoped to hear.

"I think you're right," Al replied.

"I'm glad you think so," said Ben-Gurion. "We'll expect you to come back to Israel to build one for us."

Ben-Gurion returned shortly after to Israel, where he began to have initial conversations with his military advisors and cabinet about pursuing our aviation effort. Not long after, he sent a cable to New York: it was time for Al to go to Israel—and it was time for me to come home, too.

I was eager to return—to shift from one ambitious mission to another, even grander one (though I was admittedly disappointed to be doing so just a few credits shy of my degree). As Sonia and I packed our bags, we reminisced about our time in the city—what a blessing it had been for both of us. We knew in some ways it would be hard to leave, and we expected we'd return to visit. But as bittersweet as leaving New York would be, it was nothing compared to the excitement with which we imagined stepping back onto Israeli soil.

Back home Al and I took meetings with military leaders who, as expected, were certain that such a program was a folly. The chief of the air force thought the idea ludicrous, that Israel had neither the need nor the capacity to do what we described. We met with economists and industry experts who thought it laughable that we would ever be able to export planes to foreign markets; they were convinced that the world would look with a skeptical eye on any Israeli-made products. "Our only industry is bicycles," one shouted, "and you must know it recently shut down! What madness is it to think we can build planes when we can't even build bicycles?"

We spoke to engineers who were certain that Israel lacked the expertise needed to build and manage such a complicated operation. We spoke to cabinet ministers who fumed about costs.

"With what money shall we pay for this?" one minister barked. "Israel isn't America, in case you have forgotten. We don't have the budget. We don't have the manpower. And we certainly don't have the need!"

In almost every meeting, we found the same set of circumstances—a courteous but firm dismissiveness. "The idea was too big to be true," I wrote many years ago, "and nebulous enough for them to try and stifle it on the spot." And yet I knew that we would never achieve great things if we let austerity become an obstacle to audacity. To build a stronger, more prosperous state, we had to set our gaze higher than our temporary limitations.

In normal circumstances, these reactions would have been the likely deathblow, delivered before we'd even begun. But in those days, Ben-Gurion had extraordinary influence, and could exert enormous pressure. I pleaded with him to do so in this case. What he offered was far more than I had expected. He not only agreed to move the project forward, but also told me I was expected to oversee it myself. I was just twenty-nine years old, and suddenly I was being appointed deputy director of the Defense Ministry.

In January 1952, my family and I returned from the States and moved into a small apartment in Tel Aviv. Two months later, Sonia gave birth to our first son, Yoni. It was a time of celebration and anticipation. At home, I had a beautiful family and incredible love. At work, I spent my days side by side with my mentor and hero, who gave me his blessing to chase an improbable plan.

We faced repeated obstacles. I'll never forget the day that the Ministry of Finance told us that they would be cutting our initial budget in half. What a shortsighted decision it was, and a symptom of a dangerous way of thinking—for a young country or a young business. When you are small and weak, you must ask: What kind of investments will let you grow? "Investments" can mean many things: time, money, and—perhaps the most important of all—heart. So many times in our lives we struggle to confidently leap forward, averse to the possibility that we will fall flat. Yet this fear of taking risks can be the greatest risk of all.

Of course, when you are part of a team, others might have an apprehensive veto power. What then? Rather than shutter our effort, I searched for another way. I'd come to believe that when you have two alternatives, the first thing you must do is look for a third—the one you didn't think of, that doesn't yet exist. Within my authority, I set aside a modest amount of defense ministry funds to make up for a fraction of the shortfall. Then I reached out to private donors, people who instinctively knew the necessity of the risk I wanted to take. We raised millions of dollars from those channels, allowing us to work around bureaucratic resistance and jump-start our initiative. We named the company Bedek Aviation, which means "maintenance" in Hebrew, and started construction on our first hangars in 1954.

Breaking ground didn't stop the criticism. Nor did the maintenance work we started before even finishing construction. Still, from the moment we began our work, I knew we would succeed. And within five years, when the aircraft industry became Israel's largest employer, the wilting criticism trailed off into a quiet murmur on the margins. The idea, born in the skies, was well on its way.

In 1959, we would manufacture our first aircraft, which would be used to defend the state during the Six-Day War. In time, we would realize even the most ambitious parts of our vision, building aircraft we would export all over the world—in recent years, even to Russia. Decades after Al first started wielding his wrench, the Israeli aviation industry would be renamed Israel Aerospace Industries (IAI), to commemorate the addition of space satellites to its product line. Today, most countries around the world use satellite services, but Israel remains one of a small handful capable of launching their own satellites into orbit.

But in those early months, I was reminded that the aircraft industry was a solution to only some of our problems. The planes lining up for repair looked more like they belonged in an aviation history museum than in a maintenance shop—a curated collection of retired aircraft from all over the world not intended to return to the sky. The question I had considered over Newfoundland—of how to make our security sustainable—had only been partially answered. In the meantime, we remained vulnerable.

I wrestled with the question interminably in the early 1950s—even more so when Ben-Gurion took a brief hiatus from government in 1954. He was understandably exhausted from the years of fighting, both physical and intellectual, and had chosen to retire to Kibbutz Sde Boker in the desert of the Negev. At the time, we didn't know that his retirement would only last little more than a year; we thought, perhaps, the Old Man was finished forever. Before he left, Ben-Gurion made his minister without portfolio, Pinhas Lavon, the new defense minister and me the director general of the Defense Ministry. Moshe Dayan was appointed as its chief of staff. Foreign Minister Moshe Sharett became prime minister.

There are few people I have ever known whom I admired as much as Moshe Dayan. He was a brilliant military strategist and one of my closest friends. But it weighed on us both to know that Ben-Gurion would no longer be at our side—and that he had placed in our hands the task of defending Israel from annihilation. This was the reality that kept me at the office late into the evening, and sleepless for so many nights at home. At least we'd had his leadership while struggling to build our military capacity. Without it, my confidence that I could find a reliable source of arms before we again came under attack plummeted.

What we needed, I knew, was a partner—an *ally*. The closest thing we had to a functional international alliance was our shadowy relationship with Czechoslovakia, which was based entirely on military purchasing and kept secret from the world. In some ways we had taken great pride in going it alone, building our state from the ground up partly as proof that despite our persecution, we Jews were not beaten down. All along we would have accepted the friendship of other nations, but by now it was clear that they were not going to make the effort; we were. We needed to change our standing in the world, to be seen in the eyes of other countries as a friend.

For a state of fewer than two million people, the idea of standing shoulder to shoulder with the world's major powers demanded chutzpah, to be sure. We could not be seen as a mere vassal, but as a sovereign state. But the British still treated Israel with distrust and ill will, holding firm on their embargo to sell weapons to the Middle East. In recognizing Israel, the United States had given Israel legitimacy in its most important hour. But President Dwight Eisenhower didn't want to involve the United States in the Arab-Israeli conflict, preferring that his country maintain a neutral position. It was a settled matter—and would be for some time. We were engaged in an uncertain fight for our lives—for the very existence of a Jewish state—and we were doing so while the world closed its doors to us. In this essential pursuit of an ally, it seemed there was only one possibility. After much consideration, I set my sights on France.

Like the British and the Americans, the French had an embargo in place. But I suspected we could find an emotional connection with the French, one that might persuade them to help us in secret. The Radical Party, which controlled French government in those years, had as its leaders many heroes from the Resistance who had lived under the brutal clutch of Nazi occupation. Some had been in concentration camps themselves. Our scars were not the same, but they were caused by the same evil. In this, I hoped we might find common bond.

I also saw practical reasons why France might abide. Their private defense industry manufactured a wide range of weapons, including airplanes and tanks, and Israel represented a potential new customer. Furthermore, Gamal Abdel Nasser, Egypt's president, had become a threat to us both, as Egypt was now funneling weapons to rebels in Algeria, which was still a French colony at the time. Nasser, meanwhile, was still speaking of the great virtue of destroying the State of Israel and ordering regular incursions on our border. If a common bond were insufficient, I thought we might find alliance with France over common cause.

Ben-Gurion had always been skeptical about any partnership with France. "The French?!" he would yell, every time I mentioned them. "The French? They lost the war! Ask them why they lost the war. I want to know."

"I checked on it, and I have my conclusions," I replied. "The enemy didn't cooperate."

Now that he had left for Sde Boker, I met a similar reaction from Sharett and Lavon. Lavon called the French strategy "silly." Any effort not focused on changing the minds of the British and Americans was a waste of time, he argued.

In Jerusalem, I had the support and confidence of Moshe Dayan, but of nobody else. I definitely lacked the backing of the Foreign Ministry, which under normal circumstances would have taken the lead on all such international outreach. And yet I was still alit by the spark of imagination. Despite the obstacles, off I went.

. . .

When I first left for Paris, I didn't speak a word of French or know anything about French custom and style. I was unkempt and ill-equipped, on an errand that seemed designed by a fool—that is, myself. And yet I boarded the plane filled with hope, eager to see if I could arrange what everyone else declared impossible. Soon after arriving, I phoned the office of the deputy prime minister, Paul Reynaud, whom I knew to be in charge of foreign arms sales. I told him, through a translator, that I was in town and hoped we could speak. He invited me to his office straightaway.

We had a warm and winding conversation—and a productive one at that. By the time we were finished, he was ready to sell Israel long-range cannons. We would need a great deal more than that, to be sure, but an agreement of this nature was still a watershed moment. It was our first arms deal with a major world power—and the first of many steps we would take toward genuine alliance. What else could I feel but elation?

I got up from my chair and shook hands with Reynaud, thanking him for his empathy and assistance. As he escorted me to the door of his office, I paused, suddenly struck with a question.

"*Monsieur,* I realize I haven't any idea how one government pays another." I suggested that I would deposit $1 million in a French Ministry of Defense bank account, and we could settle the balance later. Reynaud agreed.

Over the course of the next several years, I traveled back and forth between Israel and France many times to purchase arms and equipment for the IDF. I met with generals, with political officials, with members of the French cabinet. With the help of an Algerian Jew named Georges Elgosi, an economist in the French prime minister's office, I convinced the French government to supply us with several types of fighter aircraft, all of which would be crucial to winning the Six-Day War in 1967. Upon meeting me, Elgosi had decided to invite me to his apartment, where his elderly mother would have the chance, quite literally, to inspect me. I remember her sitting mysteriously in the living room, as though it were her court. When I introduced myself, she asked that I give her my hand. She examined the lines and the creases of my palm as though she were reading a map of my soul. When she finished she looked up at her son and said four simple words: "Do whatever he asks." Elgosi took his mother's conclusion to heart, it seemed. The next day, he offered me use of his office, a stone's throw away from that of Prime Minister Pierre Mendès-France. Through Elgosi, I was granted entrée into the world of French politics, where I befriended dozens of French leaders, including the prime minister himself.

I arrived without a word of French, with empty pockets, without any understanding of French culture or courtesy, but instead of condescending and rejecting such a wayward soul, the French leadership adopted me like a lost child. They brought me into their most intimate French circles, introducing me to the country's greatest politicians and generals and authors and artists. In me they saw a version of themselves, from which we formed an indescribable bond. This was not merely personal: the German occupation had not only been a political crisis but an existential one. For a people who had long thought deeply about what it meant to be French, the occupation and legacy of collaboration had forced a crisis of the soul, and in Israel's struggles Mendès-France and others may have recognized a similar pull to confront the wounds of the past.

The only barrier between our new friendship was language. During my first trips to the country, I needed a translator to join me. But soon I started using those flights as a chance to learn French myself, studying it intensively, practicing conversations with our French ambassador, and sometimes with myself. In time, I would no longer need a translator.

During one of my trips to Paris, I was invited to dinner at the home of the French army's chief of staff. I was seated next to his wife. Before the meal began, she turned to me, speaking in a whisper.

"Mr. Peres, may I suggest that you will not need to justify your intentions to me," she said.

"Pardon?"

"I don't need a word of explanation for why you are here or what you are fighting for."

"Why is that?" I asked.

She paused for a moment, as though she were searching for the right words. She pushed up the sleeve of her blouse to reveal her forearm, then twisted it ever so slightly to reveal her answer. She had been stamped and numbered like cattle, tattooed by the Nazis at a concentration camp. She was a survivor.

My efforts in France were not happening in a vacuum. At home, the tensions along our borders were worsening, particularly with Egypt. Nasser was supporting units of terrorists in Gaza. Known as the Fedayeen, the assailants had been sneaking across the border and attacking civilians. Each time we were attacked, we retaliated, but with each retaliation, it seemed, came another attack. The escalation of tension made war feel inevitable, all the more so as our intelligence reports revealed that the Egyptians were developing attack plans.

Our concerns turned existential when, in September 1955, we

learned that Nasser had just signed a major arms deal with Czechoslovakia, our once and brief partner. The agreement included hundreds of aircraft, tanks, submarines, and destroyers, along with countless crates of heavy artillery and ammunition. It was enough to make Egypt a military powerhouse overnight, enough to give Nasser's threats to annihilate Israel the gnashing teeth of credibility. A month later, in a provocative act, Nasser closed our most vital shipping route, the Straits of Tiran.

By this point, Ben-Gurion had returned to government and was once again prime minister and defense minister. He considered the closing of the straits an act of war in itself and proposed a plan to use force to reopen it. But the cabinet was skeptical, with a majority voting against it. For the time anyway, the provocation went unanswered.

In the meantime, I worried about the French. Having forged our partnership, I wondered how I would sustain it over time, especially given its mottled set of internal political partnerships and antagonisms. The French government had developed a pattern of falling suddenly and with some regularity, shifting sometimes wildly between ideological extremes. Elections had been called for January 1956, and I wondered if the Radical Party's government could survive.

I decided to spend the next several months waging my own private campaign in Paris. I ventured to build relationships with the opposition, to protect our interests should they soon take over the reins of government. The most important of those meetings was a private dinner at a small Parisian café with the head of the opposition himself—a fascinating character named Guy Mollet.

Mollet was a socialist, as, he knew, was I. In fact, when I first sat down to the table, he greeted me as "comrade," and we bonded quite sincerely over the worldview we shared. Eventually, we got down to business.

"What is it that you want?" he asked.

I told him the story or our work with the Radicals and was honest with him about my worries. Though I sympathized with his ideological viewpoint, I expressed fear that Israel would be made vulnerable were he to take over the French government.

Mollet listened intently and engaged me thoughtfully over a meal with many courses and many glasses of wine. By the end of the dinner, he made me a promise. "If I shall be elected," he said, "I shall answer your call of assistance."

While appreciative of the sentiment, I remained visibly skeptical.

"Why do you doubt this?" he asked.

"It's not that I doubt you, personally," I said. "But I know the socialists. When you're in the opposition, you promise the world. But when you come to power, you forget your promises."

"Who did this to you?"

I told him the story of the English politician Ernest Bevin. While in the opposition, Bevin had been a good friend to Israel. But once he became foreign minister, Bevin became a great enemy instead, enforcing the White Paper of 1939, even after the British technically had rescinded it.

"I shall not be Bevin," Mollet responded. "You can count on me."

On January 2, 1956, I learned that I would indeed need to count on him. The Radical Party had lost the elections and Mollet was charged with forming a government. I was stunned and, despite our warm conversation, quite worried about his willingness—and ability—to ultimately follow through.

Within a few months, I put his promise to the test. It was well after midnight when I received an urgent call, requesting that I come to Ben-Gurion's office at once. The clashes with the Egyptian Army in Gaza were getting worse, and we feared Nasser was readying a full-scale attack.

"I need you to go to France right away," Ben-Gurion told me. "I have a letter for you to give to Mollet. See if you can get him to help us." The letter described our concerns about Nasser, that he appeared to have access to a practically unlimited supply of Soviet arms, and that his actions represented "a terrifying threat to the State of Israel." Ben-Gurion asked for France's emergency assistance—making clear that without Mollet's support, Israel's very survival was at stake.

I boarded a plane and was soon sitting across from Guy Mollet once again, this time at the Hotel Matignon, the prime minister's official residence. I pleaded my case. "I believe you have nothing to worry about. We can help you," he said. He saw the relief in my eyes on hearing the news, and whispered one more thing to me. "Didn't I tell you I wouldn't be Bevin?" he asked with a grin and a wink.

In June 1956, Moshe Dayan and I returned to Paris for a meeting with senior military leadership. Dayan made a poised and passionate case that Nasser could soon attack Israel, and raised the possibility of a joint operation with the French. "We shall be ready to act together with you against Nasser," he explained, "to the extent that you will be ready to cooperate with us." The French officers in attendance agreed—at least in principle.

"If we are to be prepared," I interjected, "then we must be rearmed. It is the only way." I handed the officers a wish list of the weaponry and equipment we needed, having inflated the amounts to give myself room for negotiation. To my great shock, the officers didn't flinch, or make any effort to counter.

We returned home feeling a greater sense of confidence, and soon began receiving the new weapons from France. We continued to monitor Nasser's troop movements, while staving off more border incursions. Then, in July 1956, Nasser announced a fateful decision: he intended to nationalize the Suez Canal.

The canal had been operated by the Suez Canal Company, a joint enterprise of the British and French, both of whom used the trade route to transport oil and other essential goods. Having Egypt take control of the canal thus represented a grave economic danger to both Western powers. The French had already been ready to go to war with Nasser. Now the British were similarly inclined.

I was in Paris when Nasser made his announcement, and I spent the next day in meetings with the French defense minister, Maurice Bourgès-Maunoury. I returned to Israel the following afternoon and was picked up by Ben-Gurion and Moshe Dayan at the airport. On our drive to Jerusalem, I briefed them both on the conversations. I told them that the French and the British were both interested in joining forces with Israel to remove the Egyptian threat. The British were willing, so long as Israel committed not to attack Jordan, with whom the British had a treaty. Beyond the details of the campaign itself, which had yet to be determined, there remained a question of timing. The French favored immediate action, while the British preferred two more months to seek a political resolution. Ben-Gurion generally favored the contours of the conversation, though he remained skeptical about the British joining the fight. As to the timing, he preferred the French call for immediacy given the likelihood of an Egyptian attack.

I returned to France shortly after to continue our discussions—to move beyond the general question of whether we would go to war together and into the details of how we would execute the campaign. I was accompanied by Golda Meir, who had recently been named foreign minister. Golda viewed me as one of her greatest annoyances. She was frustrated that I had managed to earn the trust of Ben-Gurion—a man whom she worshipped as the singular figure he was. She was frustrated that he listened to my ideas, even the ones she thought were reckless or fantastical. She was frustrated that I built our relationship with the French outside of the Foreign Ministry, where such a thing would normally take place. I suppose I empathized with her, even while she treated me with such suspicion. She had been at Ben-Gurion's side for years and I had only just arrived. Were I in her position, I imagined I, too, would have been upset.

Our first meeting in France didn't improve the situation between us. To our surprise, Guy Mollet didn't attend, which frustrated Golda, heightening both her suspicions about the chance of military cooperation and her general disdain for me. But it was upon hearing the recommended battle plan that Golda's impatience turned to fury. The proposed scenario would become known as the "Israeli pretext": the French and British wanted Israel to attack Egypt first, giving the French and British a justification to intervene in the conflict. "The Israelis will start a war with the Egyptians," one of the French attendees explained, "and then we will come to separate them. When the Israelis withdraw and the Egyptians do not, we have the pretext we need to expel them [from the Suez Canal]."

Golda found the notion preposterous—a complete nonstarter. She felt I had exaggerated France's willingness to partner with us, that I had taken us embarrassingly far down an uncertain road. And though Ben-Gurion didn't agree with Golda's assessment of me personally, he, too, was concerned about the French proposal. He feared that the "Israeli pretext" would risk our standing in the international community—that we would be viewed as the provocateur, even though Egypt had already committed at least one act of war and many more aggressions against us. In this, he was surely justified. But Moshe Dayan made a counterargument that I found quite persuasive.

"England and France don't need us," he told Ben-Gurion frankly. "They have all the aircraft they need to annihilate the Egyptian Air Force. The only advantage we have in this matter," he argued, "which is the only one England and France don't have, is our ability to give them the needed pretext to enter the campaign." Though Ben-Gurion remained skeptical, he believed a deal was still possible. It was time, he concluded, for him to go to Paris himself—to meet with the French and British in person. I cabled Paris immediately to set up the conference.

That Sunday, a plane from Paris landed in Tel Aviv to take us to the meeting. A small group of us made our way to the airport, cloaked in secrecy. Ben-Gurion wore a wide-brimmed hat to hide his signature white hair. Dayan took off his easily identifiable eye patch and wore dark sunglasses on the trip instead. (There was some irony in Dayan planning armed collaboration in this instance, since it had been a bullet from a French sniper back in 1941 that had resulted in the loss of his eye.)

When we arrived at the airport, Ben-Gurion was taken directly to the villa in Sèvres where the discussions were to take place. Nestled on the banks of the River Seine, Sèvres was a quiet town with a rich history. Despite the formality of the estate and the seriousness the moment commanded, the meeting itself was quite warm. Ben-Gurion described his objections and his demands to a group of Frenchmen who seemed to hold him in the highest regard. The back-and-forth was cordial and comfortable—a beautiful sight indeed. But when the British foreign secretary, Selwyn Lloyd, arrived, it was as if an ice storm had suddenly blown in.

From the moment Ben-Gurion and Lloyd shook hands, it was clear that neither liked the other. Lloyd was unpleasant and unfriendly, curt with his words, devoid of imagination, and, at times, openly hostile. He regarded Ben-Gurion more as a former enemy than a future ally, more a partner of necessity than choice. The feeling was mutual.

As the conference continued into its second day, Ben-Gurion had not yet decided whether he would accept any plan that required the "Israeli pretext," but the discussions of tactics continued on with the assumption that he ultimately would. There were a number of proposals batted around among us, but by the end of the session it was clear that only one was feasible. This scenario involved Israel attacking Egypt on the night of October 29, destroying the Egyptian Air Force as it worked its way to the Sinai. The next morning, France and England would demand that Israel and Egypt cease any military action and retreat from the Suez.

When Nasser predictably rejected those conditions, the French and British would launch their own assault against Egypt.

When Moshe and I left Sèvres, Ben-Gurion had yet to make up his mind. The two of us ventured down to a nearby café, where we sipped wine while discussing the choices ahead. We didn't have a good sense of Ben-Gurion's thinking, and though we were both strongly in favor of intervention, we did not take his choice lightly. It was a complicated decision with broad implications, based on an imperfect set of facts. And Ben-Gurion was forced to make it knowing that in every war, there are elements of blindness. Obviously a defeat would badly damage France and England, commercially and politically. But for us the stakes were incomprehensibly higher, both for our global standing and our own survival. In his hands Ben-Gurion held what I thought of as a "cruel watch," the hours running out fast before he had to make the decision that might be the end, not just of a country, but of the Jewish future. None of us envied him.

The next morning, we were summoned back to Sèvres. When we arrived, Ben-Gurion was sitting outside in the grand garden of the villa, under a tree. Noticing our approach, he pulled a piece of paper from his pocket on which he had written several questions for us. As he read them aloud, Moshe and I immediately realized that we had our answer. He was asking us questions about tactics and timing, about military logistics and political considerations. It was clear, by the very act of posing such questions, that Ben-Gurion was no longer ambivalent about our efforts. He had decided that Israel was going to war.

As the conversation continued, Ben-Gurion asked Moshe to draw up a map of the campaign he envisioned. But out in the garden, none of us had any paper, so I pulled from my pocket a pack of cigarettes and handed it to Dayan. He sketched a map of the Sinai Peninsula, and drew on it flight paths and paratrooper drop locations. When the discussion was over, the three of us realized that we had just produced the first map of what would be a historic campaign. We passed it between us and signed the sketch, which I then returned to my pocket.

Five days later, the war began.

When we first sat down to discuss a possible campaign several months earlier, the French defense minister had asked how long I thought it would take to conquer the Sinai.

"Three to four days," I told him. He was certain it would take at least three to four weeks. In the end, it took only a few hours longer than my initial estimate. The IDF marched through the Sinai with incredible speed and agility, forcing Egypt into retreat, sending massive convoys of Egyptian vehicles fleeing in the opposite direction of the fighting. Injured aircraft were repaired at our own aviation facilities, where more than one thousand people worked day and night on maintenance. It was so swift, in fact, that by the time the French and British launched their own invasions, the fighting was complete. "Total collapse of the Egyptian Army in Sinai," I cabled to Paris. "Brilliant and complete victory of the IDF on all fronts."

By the time it was over, the blockade of the Straits of Tiran had been destroyed, along with nearly all of the Egyptian Air Force. The Fedayeen bases were in shambles. The threat of imminent attack had gone.

In victory, we solidified our partnership with the French, an alliance we could come to depend on until the eve of the Six-Day War. The swift show of bravery by what some deemed "little

Israel" gave us newfound confidence and a reputation for tactical brilliance. And it gave us more than ten years without a major war.

It was, for me personally, a time of profound development—a time when wisdom was formed under extraordinary pressure, like a diamond in the depths of the earth's mantle. I learned about the virtue of imagination and the power of creative decision making. An alliance with France was my "impossible" dream, and I pursued it. The aviation industry was Al's and my "impossible" dream, and we built it together. We were quick and creative, and boldly ambitious, and in that we found our reward.

But I also learned that there is a cost to dreaming. At first it was my ideas that were ridiculed. Soon, however, it was me—and only by extension, my positions—who took most of the incoming fire. I was attacked and discounted, seen as dangerously naïve, and accused of all manner of terrible things. My detractors couldn't understand how I had managed to get into Ben-Gurion's head, or how to get me back out—as if the man they worshipped (as I also did) could be co-opted. And because so much of what I did was in secret—the arms deal, the French alliance, Suez operation—I had little choice but to live in the shadows. My critics often knew—and would only ever know—half of the story.

In this, I came to understand the choice at the heart of leadership: to pursue big dreams and suffer the consequences, or narrow one's ambitions in an effort to get along. For me, there was only one choice. I knew of no way to become someone else, and so I chose to be myself, and in doing so, to serve a cause greater than myself. I decided that accomplishment mattered more than credit, more than popularity, more than title. It was not that I didn't want those things; it was that having them in the absence of action and risk and courage would have been empty. There were easier ways to pursue mediocrity. And so I chose not to wallow or to be distracted from my dreams, but instead to think inventively and creatively about a path our young state would follow. I wanted that state to be a flourishing one, a just and peaceful and moral one. And so I let myself dream, and I refused to give in to cynicism.

Were there disappointments along the way? Of course. I've had sleepless nights and restless days because of big dreams. I've lost elections over them. I've lost some friends over them, too. But they never discouraged my imagination. Success built my confidence. Failure steeled my spine.

Experience has taught me three things about cynicism: First, it's a powerful force with the ability to trample the aspirations of an entire people. Second, it is universal, fundamentally part of human nature, a disease that is ubiquitous and global. Third, it is the single greatest threat to the next generation of leadership. In a world of so many grave challenges, what could be more dangerous than discouraging ideas and ambition?

Throughout my life, I have been accused by many people (in many languages) of being too optimistic—of having too rosy a view of the world and the people who inhabit it. I tell them that both optimists and pessimists die in the end, but the optimist leads a hopeful and happy existence while the pessimist spends his days cynical and downtrodden. It is too high a price to pay.

Besides, optimism is a prerequisite of progress. It provides the inspiration we need, especially in hard times. And it provides the encouragement that wills us to chase our grandest ambitions out into the world, instead of locking them away in the safe quiet of our minds.

CHAPTER 3

THE LEGEND AND
LEGACY OF DIMONA

On the morning of September 13, 1993, I stood with a small group in a round, windowless room with walls covered in an intricate mural. As the antique clock struck eleven, we were given instructions to line up in procession. We were about to sign a historic document—the first declaration of principles of peace between Israelis and Palestinians—and the ceremony was about to begin. I exchanged warm greetings with former U.S. presidents George H. W. Bush and Jimmy Carter, who were standing just in front of me, and who had both played a role in the long path to peace. Behind me were President Bill Clinton, Chairman Yasser Arafat, and Prime Minister Yitzhak Rabin, preparing to make a historic commitment to peace.

"Ladies and Gentlemen, the Vice President of the United States, Albert Gore Jr.; His Excellency, Shimon Peres, Minister of Foreign Affairs of Israel; Mr. Abbas, Member of the Executive Council of the Palestine Liberation Organization."

We stepped out of the White House and onto the sweeping South Lawn, an audience of thousands gathered before us, along with television cameras and reporters from news outlets around the world. As we made our way to the stage where President Clinton would soon welcome us to an occasion of "history and hope," I thought back to the first decision that had started us down this long, uncertain path toward peace. Not the decision to reach out to the Palestinians in secret, nor our previous attempts to negotiate with our enemies. In that moment, my mind turned to a time nearly forty years earlier—a time when Ben-Gurion and I swam alone in a sea of opposition.

It was October 24, 1956, at the villa in Sèvres where the French and Israeli leadership were meeting to finalize the plans for Operation Suez. Ben-Gurion and I stood in one of the mansion's sweeping spaces; it was at once a ballroom, an art museum, and a well-stocked saloon. Across the way, French foreign minister Christian Pineau and defense minister Maurice Bourgès-Maunoury were deep in conversation, but otherwise unoccupied. I sensed an opportunity, perhaps the perfect moment.

I turned to Ben-Gurion and said in the quietest whisper, "I think I can get it done now." He gave me a subtle nod of agreement. I took a deep, steeling breath.

I approached the two gentlemen, who by then were dear friends, and raised an issue that caught both by surprise. I had come over to discuss one of Israel's most ambitious aspirations: to enter the nuclear age. To do so, we would need something from France— something no country in history had ever given another.

Our interest in nuclear energy was not new. It had been a subject of great intellectual curiosity for Ben-Gurion and myself long before that fateful moment in Sèvres. Neither of us was an expert regarding nuclear energy; at best, we were enthusiasts. But we both saw great potential in its peaceful pursuit. For his part, Ben-Gurion believed that only science could compensate for what nature had denied us. Israel had no oil, and it lacked access to sufficient fresh water; nuclear energy held the potential to solve both problems—countries like France were using it not only to create a reliable energy source, but also as a means of desalinating salt water. He also believed, as I did, that there existed great intellectual and economic value at the frontier of technology. By making investments in the cutting edge of science, by building talent and expertise at our universities, we believed we could invigorate the untapped minds of a nation.

There was great power in this idea, to be sure. But in truth, it was a political motivation, more than a scientific one, that animated my interest. If we were to succeed in building a reactor, our enemies would never believe its purpose to be peaceful. Israel was already viewed with such intense suspicion by those opposed to our existence that I was certain neither public statements nor private assurances nor even the presentation of concrete evidence would sway skeptics from believing that we possessed the capacity for nuclear war. As Thomas Hobbes wrote in *Leviathan,* the "reputation of power is power." My theory was its corollary: The reputation of nuclear is deterrence. And deterrence, I believed, was the first step on the path toward peace.

At the time, the Arab world had made commitments to Israel's annihilation a litmus test for leadership; indeed, every Middle Eastern politician or general who hoped to ascend had to prove he was more intent on destroying us than his rival was. I believed that sowing doubt in their ability to actually do so was our highest security imperative.

Over time, my conversations with Ben-Gurion shifted from the theoretical to the practical. If we were to even entertain such an effort, we intended to understand exactly what it would require. First, it was to be a massive undertaking—both in terms of the scale of the construction and the scientific capability it required. Second, Israel lacked the raw materials and the engineering experience required to build a reactor. At the same time, we well understood that cutting corners was not an option, either—with nuclear energy, compromise and catastrophe are one and the same.

What we needed was help, and as the country with whom we'd built our closest friendship, France represented an opportunity. As Europe's most advanced country in the nuclear field, it also represented our best option. Indeed, the French industry had built teams of engineers and scientists with precise expertise. France's universities were the best place in the world to study nuclear physics. They had at their disposal everything we would need to build a nuclear reactor.

Ben-Gurion had decided it would not be enough for me to raise the issue with the French. I had to make an explicit request: to sell Israel a nuclear reactor for peaceful purposes. It was a request without precedent, and one I expected my friends to decline. They were already taking a great risk violating the Western arms embargo to sell us weapons in secret. But something of this magnitude, if discovered, was far more dangerous, with the potential to damage French relations with both its Arab partners and its Western allies. Still, I felt that if such an agreement were possible between any countries, it was possible between France and Israel. And so I set out to try.

TOP: My grandfather Meltzer and his descendants in Vishneva, Poland, 1923. I'm standing third from the right in the back row. *GPO*

BOTTOM: Me *(on the right)*; my brother, Gershon (Gigi); and our parents, Sarah and Yitzhak Persky, in Vishneva, 1928. *Shimon Peres Archives*

The *Tarbut* School in Vishneva, 1931. I'm sitting on the left in the front row.
Shimon Peres Archives

TOP: Fourteen years old, a teenager in the land of our forefathers, with the birth of the State of Israel still more than a decade away. *Shimon Peres Archives*

BOTTOM: Newly wed with Sonia in Tel Aviv, May 1945. *Shimon Peres Archives*

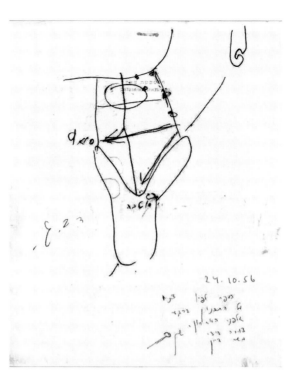

TOP: Our plan for the Sinai operation in 1956, drawn by Moshe Dayan and signed by David Ben-Gurion. *Courtesy of the I.D.F and Defense Establishment Archives*

BOTTOM: Sonia, Tsvia, Yonatan (Yoni), and I admire baby Nechemia (Chemi), 1958. *Avraham Vered, in* Bamahane *magazine, courtesy of the I.D.F and Defense Establishment Archives*

With Prime Minister David Ben-Gurion in Dimona in the late 1950s.
Shimon Peres Archives

Prime Minister Yitzhak Rabin and I welcome the hostages after Operation
Entebbe. *Uri Herzl Tzahik, courtesy of the I.D.F and Defense Establishment Archives*

Speaking with the hostages after Operation Entebbe. *Uri Herzl Tzahik, courtesy of the I.D.F and Defense Establishment Archives*

Meeting with Egyptian president Anwar Sadat in the city of Beersheba, 1979.
Nati Harnik/GPO

With the chairman of the Histadrut, Yisrael Kessar, as he signs the 1985 Economic Stabilization Plan, alongside the minister of finance, Yitzhak Modai, and the minister of the economy, Gad Yaacobi. *Nati Harnik/GPO*

Signing the Oslo Accords in Washington, D.C., September 1993.
Avi Ohayon/GPO

LEFT: One of my proudest achievements as prime minister during the mid-1980s was Operation Moses, a secret effort to bring Ethiopian Jews to safety in Israel. Of the approximately 8,000 we rescued, 1,500 were children. *Nati Harnik/GPO*

ABOVE: With Prime Minister Yitzhak Rabin and Palestinian Authority Chairman Yasser Arafat, as we receive the Nobel Peace Prize in October 1994.
Sa'ar Ya'acov/GPO

RIGHT: Greeting Pope Francis on the airport tarmac during his visit to Israel.
Avi Ohayon/GPO

TOP: With German chancellor Angela Merkel in Berlin. *Amos Ben Gershom/GPO*

BOTTOM: Launching my Facebook page alongside the company's founder, Mark Zuckerberg, at Facebook's headquarters in California, 2012. *Moshe Milner/GPO*

Receiving the Presidential Medal of Freedom from President Barack Obama, June 2012. *Amos Ben Gershom/GPO*

At our national ceremony for outstanding soldiers at the President's Residence on Independence Day, 2013. *Amos Ben Gershom/GPO*

After their momentary shock at my question, Pineau and Bourgès-Maunoury excused themselves to the other side of the villa to discuss the matter in private. The timing of the request was not a coincidence, and I suspected they understood this. At the very same moment, Moshe Dayan was in an adjacent room with his French and British counterparts, drafting the Sèvres Protocol, which would govern the Sinai campaign, including the requirement that we attack first. We all knew that Ben-Gurion had agreed to that plan only at the urging of the French. I wanted Bourgès-Maunoury and Pineau to remember that, and to consider it when weighing the risks inherent in my request of them.

A few moments later, the two returned. To my utter surprise, they nodded in agreement.

"I am ready to draft the agreement right away," said Pineau.

. . .

While we had the unanimous support of the French senior leadership, we arrived back in Jerusalem to find near-unanimous dissent. Golda Meir insisted that such a project would hurt Israel's relationship with the United States, while Isser Harel, the Mossad chief, raised fears of a Soviet response. Some predicted an invasion by ground forces, while others envisioned an attack from the air. The head of the foreign relations committee said he feared the project would be "so expensive that we shall be left without bread and even without rice"—an acknowledgment that in the age of austerity, we were still struggling to feed our people. For his part, Levi Eshkol, then the finance minister, promised we wouldn't see a penny from him. Among the group, there was disagreement only about which disastrous outcome was most likely.

The response was no more encouraging within the scientific community. Israel's physicists voiced objections to entangling scientific work with government action, which they feared would stifle their research work and harm their international reputations. But more to the point, they argued that such a pursuit was both unwise and impractical. How naïve they thought I was for believing a state so small could undertake a task so large. This was not vision, it was delusion, and they would have nothing to do with it. When I approached the Weizmann Institute, the most prestigious institute in all of Israel, the head of the physics department said I was dreaming irresponsibly, that surely such an effort would lead Israel down a dark and dangerous path. He made sure I understood that his institute would play no role in whatever I intended.

Innovation, I have come to understand, is always an uphill climb. But rarely does it find so many obstacles arrayed against it at all once. We had no money, no engineers, no support from the physics community or the cabinet or the military leadership or the opposition. "What are we going to do?" Ben-Gurion asked me late one night, as we sat quietly in his office. It was the operative question. What we had was a French promise—only that, and each other.

I was often reminded about how unusual my relationship with Ben-Gurion had become—how rare it was to have a prime minister place so much trust in a young man with a junior title. Again and again, he had taken a risk in putting me in charge of important and controversial projects. And so while the reasonable answer to his question would have been to admit defeat, I decided that I owed it to him to find another way. Failing honestly and with integrity was something I could accept—but only if I was sure that my efforts to succeed had been worthy of the trust he had placed in me. In this case, that trust was so vast that, rather than surrender, I proposed an alternative plan.

That plan drew upon my experience with Al Schwimmer. The lack of public resources could be made up for with private resources, I argued. And with the right kind of recruiting effort, I believed we could build a team of Israeli engineers who could work alongside their French counterparts.

"If we fail to secure the money and the team, we can accept defeat," I said. "Until then, I think it would be foolish not to make the attempt."

Ben-Gurion agreed. "Go then," he told me. "Give order to the story."

We took to the phones and made passionate, personal (and highly confidential) appeals to some of Israel's most reliable donors from around the world. In short order, we had raised enough money to cover half the cost of the reactor—more than enough to start building our team.

We were lucky to count Yisrael Dostrovsky as one of our early members. A decorated Israeli scientist, Dostrovsky had invented a process for manufacturing heavy water and sold it to the French years earlier. But even he could not compete with the brilliance of Ernst David Bergmann, whom I approached to join the mission. In 1934, legend has it, Chaim Weizmann sought Albert Einstein's recommendation for a scientist to lead his newly created institute outside Tel Aviv. Einstein gave him only one name—that of Ernst

Bergmann, who had earned his total confidence. As one of Israel's only physicists in favor of our efforts, he would quickly earn my confidence, as well.

With Bergmann and Dostrovsky, we had scientific know-how. But what we needed even more was a project manager whom we could trust with such a delicate task. We needed a pedantic stickler, someone allergic to compromise—especially given the dangers involved in radioactive work. And yet we also needed someone who was agile, someone willing to take on a project for which he would certainly lack expertise. There was a natural tension that existed between those requirements, one that quickly whittled down my list of candidates to one.

Manes Pratt was a decorated academic with a wealth of real-world experience. We met during the War of Independence, when we worked together on the frantic building up of the IDF. He was consistently and insistently precise, the kind of man for whom perfection is not a distant pursuit, but a minimum ante. He was quick-footed and quick-witted, and he demanded in those around him the same relentless work ethic he practiced.

When I explained my proposal and the position I wanted him to consider, he looked as though he could have struck me. He couldn't disguise his disbelief.

"Are you crazy?" he demanded. "I don't have the slightest idea what it would take to build a reactor. I don't know how it looks; I don't even know what it is! How could you expect me to take charge of such a project?"

"Manes, look: I know that you don't know anything yet. But if there is somebody in this country who can become an expert after studying it for three months, that person is clearly you."

His agitation started to subside. "And what exactly would that entail?"

I suggested that we would send him to France for three months to study nuclear reactors alongside the experts who would help us build one. And I promised that if he returned to Israel after that time still uncomfortable with his fluency in the topic, he could simply return to his previous work. With no requirement for a permanent commitment, Pratt ultimately agreed. And to no one's surprise, when he returned from France, he did so as the finest nuclear expert we would ever come to know.

With the leadership in place, I turned to the work of building the rest of the team. I knew that the older generation of physicists was deeply opposed to our efforts, but I suspected that we could find students and young graduates who were eager to pursue such an ambitious project. Having been turned away by the Weizmann Institute, I turned to the Israeli Institute of Technology, in Haifa, known as the Technion. There I found a group of scientists and engineers who were eager to take the leap alongside us. Like Pratt, I intended to send each Technion recruit to France for a period of study.

The next part of the challenge lay less in convincing the young scientists to sign up and more in helping them convince their own families. We intended to locate the reactor in the Negev, near Beersheba, which at the time was like the end of the world. The young Israeli families were understandably reluctant to leave the modern cities of Haifa and Tel Aviv for a harsh and distant desert. And if this was how the Israelis felt, I suspected the French contractors would be apoplectic. So I pledged to them not just to build an industrial facility, but to build a community—indeed, a whole separate suburb in Beersheba with all they needed for a high quality of life: good schools, a modern hospital, a shopping court—even a hair salon.

After some reluctance, the families put their trust in me and the work began. The students went off to France to study nuclear engineering—and I joined them, not as the leader of the project but as a peer. Chemistry and nuclear physics were challenging subjects, to be sure, and I came to them without any previous training. But I felt it essential to gain a degree of mastery in the science that would be driving the project. In previous endeavors, I had come to understand that in addition to a clear vision and strategy, true leadership requires intricate knowledge—a facility with the granular details of every aspect of the mission. If I were to lead a group of scientists and engineers, I had an obligation to understand the work I was asking them to undertake. And so, alongside these young physicists, I spent day and night studying atomic particles and nuclear energy, and the process required to harness its power.

Funds and scientists in place, what remained was the work of formalizing the partnership with France. We had signed an initial agreement laying out our intentions in broad terms, but there were still details requiring discussion. In the summer of 1957, I flew to Paris to begin making arrangements.

When I arrived, Bourgès-Maunoury was the newly minted prime minister. Guy Mollet's government had fallen in June. For Israel, there was serendipity in the timing. Though Mollet had always been a generous and reliable partner, I had developed an especially close friendship with Bourgès-Maunoury. His sense of humor could be grim and cynical, but in truth he was as hopeful an optimist as I, and he consistently looked upon Israel with an instinctive sense of obligation. His support for the Jewish state resided somewhere deep in his soul, and I felt there was nothing of him I could not ask.

Together we worked through other agreements, which outlined the ways our two nations would cooperate. Bourgès-Maunoury was supportive, but Pineau, who by then had become foreign minister, had raised concerns about the proposed wording. I was sure that, in normal circumstances, Pineau and I could find common ground and common language—that his concerns could be relieved quite easily through compromise. But just as we were processing the substance of Pineau's objections, Bourgès-Maurnoury's government, just formed, began to crumble. For Israel, this was nothing short of a crisis. We needed to secure support from both men before they no longer had the power to provide it.

I was in Israel when I learned the French parliament was preparing a vote of no confidence in Bourgès-Maunoury, and set off for Paris at once. By the time I arrived, it was clear the government would fall the following night. I had just one day—to persuade Pineau to agree to the proposed arrangement, to secure the necessary two signatures, to end the crisis, and to save the program. I was suddenly a witness to and participant in one of the greatest dramas of my life.

I started with Pineau. When I arrived at his office, it was clear he had been expecting me. He greeted me kindly but wasted no time informing me that his position was final, and that he was firmly opposed to the agreement as worded. His concerns were largely based in a fear that the agreement would become public. I pleaded with him to give me a final chance to persuade him. Out of respect for our long-standing friendship, he obliged.

I responded as thoroughly as I could. I spoke from the heart about the genuine anguish I felt for my state. I wanted to be sure he understood the power he held in his hands, and the consequence of his decision, one way or the other. This was not a moment that would be forgotten; it was one upon which history would hinge.

Finally, he spoke.

"I accept your arguments, Shimon," he declared to my utter surprise. "You've convinced me."

It was an unexpected and energizing victory, but with time running short, I knew that Pineau's acquiescence was insufficient to secure the deal on its own. I pressed for urgency.

"What is your consent worth after the government falls? Perhaps you could call Bourgès-Maunoury. He needs to hear it from you."

Pineau agreed, but he was unable to reach Bourgès-Maunoury. We learned he was in session, presiding over his final cabinet meeting. With Bourgès-Maunoury behind closed doors, there was no way I could get to him before the government fell.

I refused to accept this. "Give me your consent in writing, then, and I'll bring it to Bourgès-Maunoury straightaway!"

Pineau obliged, though he seemed convinced the exercise was futile. I thanked him for his extraordinary effort and friendship, then raced for the door.

I arrived at parliament out of breath and undeterred. I didn't know how I'd get to Bourgès-Maunoury, but I hoped an answer would reveal itself. And indeed, as I headed up the stairs of the French parliament, the answer was heading down them: it was an aide to Bourgès-Maunoury, one I had come to know well over the years. He recognized me and greeted me in French. I explained the situation in all its stressful detail, then scribbled a note to Bourgès-Maunoury quickly on a leaf of paper.

"Please deliver this to the prime minister," I asked him. "It is a matter of the greatest urgency." The aide agreed. He took the note and disappeared into the chamber while I stood anxiously awaiting a response.

A few minutes later, a voice called to me from down the hallway. "Bonjour, Shimon!" It was Bourgès-Maunoury, embattled but stoic. He explained that after reading my note, he took the unprecedented step of temporarily adjourning the meeting.

"Only for a true friend," he whispered.

I showed him the letter from Pineau and explained why the stakes were so high. I needed him to return to his meeting and get his cabinet to approve the deal before the end of the session. And I needed him to sign the authorization before his government fell. Bourgès-Maunoury promised his assistance. He would return to the meeting and get swift approval, then temporarily adjourn the meeting once again—giving him just enough time to affix his signature to the final agreement.

"Go wait for me in my office," he suggested. "I'll come find you."

And so I waited. For hours I waited. But Bourgès-Maunoury never came. He had been unable to find a way to excuse himself. The opposition had made their move on the vote of no confidence, and there was little that Bourgès-Maunoury could do to create a delay. Late into the night, the government fell. The document remained unsigned.

The next morning, I returned to Bourgès-Maunoury's office, as dejected and exhausted as he was. He was now the former prime minister. I didn't know what to say.

"I understand from you that my socialist friend has consented to the agreement."

I nodded.

"Wonderful," he said. "This should take care of it then."

He took a piece of stationery from a desk that was no longer his and drafted a letter to the chairman of the French Atomic Energy Commission. The French government had approved the deal, he confirmed, and the chairman should fully cooperate in its execution. He signed it as France's prime minister. At the top of the page, he wrote the previous day's date.

I asked no questions. I said nothing at all. What was there to say? Bourgès-Maunoury could see the relief in my eyes. He could feel the depth of my appreciation. In that moment, what he had done for Israel—what he had done for me—was the most generous display of friendship I had ever known. The following month, the French established a $10 million line of credit for Israel. At last, it was time to break ground.

. . .

On July 17, 1958, my second son, Nechemia "Chemi" Jacob, was born, marking a wonderful year for Sonia and me as we completed our family. It gave us both such fullness in our hearts.

But my work behind the scenes of government was taking some toll. In such a complex political system, it was a challenge to earn recognition or to defend my ideas and actions. As a civil servant, I was prohibited from speaking publicly, even about things that were not classified, and so I spent many days listening to critics ridicule me without being able to respond. Though it was personally hard,

I admit, it was something true leadership demanded—and I was willing to oblige.

And yet, in the late 1950s, I realized that what was lost in my silence was more than unnecessary personal vindication; it was that my essential arguments about values and motives, about a willingness to dream and the power of imagination, remained unarticulated. I had a worldview, an operating principle, one that I felt was essential to the future of the state. And though I would always remain quiet about the things that could not be said, I believed it was time to speak boldly on all of those that could. I started to consider running for the Knesset. In order to do so, I would need to resign from the ministry and reestablish my residency at Alumot. Then I would submit my candidacy to the Mapai nominating committee, which Ben-Gurion largely controlled. In the spring of 1958, I approached the Old Man with the idea, apprehensive at how he might react. To my relief, he was quite understanding. He seemed to like the idea of amplifying my voice. But he worried about my leaving.

I didn't want to leave, either. Instead, I suggested that after winning the seat, Ben-Gurion could appoint me deputy defense minister, and from that perch I could run the ministry just as I had as director general. It would be a continuation of my role, and a heavier workload, but as an elected representative, I would regain my voice. Ben-Gurion agreed that it was a good plan and gave me his blessing for the race.

In the meantime, on a plateau named Dimona in the north of the Negev, we began the tedious effort of constructing a nuclear research facility. Pratt and I commissioned the country's top architects to ensure that its form was as powerful as its function. And we put as much care into the building of the complex as we did into the building of the reactor itself.

The progress was promising. But just as I was beginning my campaign for the Knesset, another political earthquake rocked Paris. Once again, the entire program was at risk.

In the summer of 1959, General Charles de Gaulle was elected prime minister of France. His choice for foreign minister was a man named Maurice Couve de Murville, a career diplomat who was no friend of Israel. Upon learning of our nuclear partnership, Couve de Murville set out immediately to end it. After recalling the French ambassador from Tel Aviv, Couve de Murville informed Golda Meir, who was then foreign minister, that he intended to abrogate France's nuclear agreements with Israel. He expected the work to stop immediately. He was adamant, and from Golda's perspective, immovable.

I asked Ben-Gurion to send me to Paris. I intended to speak to Couve de Murville—but what to say, I did not know. I had no reason to doubt Golda's report. Perhaps Couve de Murville could be persuaded, though she certainly didn't think so. Neither, it seemed, did he. I boarded the plane depressed and frustrated, believing I'd surely return to Israel in failure. I had long believed that the best way to convince a country to work with us was not to explain how it would help Israel, but how it would help them. I needed to convince Couve de Murville that it was better for him—and for France—to keep the agreements in place. All through the journey I practiced my arguments and rehearsed possible responses, trying to concoct a way to persuade him.

When I arrived at his office, Couve de Murville welcomed me with a colorless smile, formed not in friendship, but in courtesy. He wasted no time explaining his objections and assuring me that the nuclear arrangement was finished.

"What you are proposing is to renege on France's obligations," I told him. "You are intending to breach agreements that your predecessors crafted with the force of law. And we will both be worse for it."

"How so?"

"Without these agreements in place, Israel will be left with worse than nothing. No reactor. No research facility. And no way to get back the wasted money and effort. And for France it is a problem, too," I explained. "The agreements include a commitment not to reveal the details of our work together to the Arab world. It could lead to a boycott of French companies."

At this, he interrupted. "We have no intention of violating that part of the agreement. France won't divulge anything."

"Yes, but you see," I replied, "you cannot breach your obligations to us in one part of the agreement and yet expect us to fulfill our obligations to you in the others."

It was subtle, but effective. Couve de Murville found himself contemplating a scenario he hadn't imagined. How costly would it be if the Arab world turned on France?

"What are you proposing?" he asked, in a newly cautious tone.

"France can end the agreement from this moment on, but you have no right to abrogate any of the decisions retroactively," I insisted. "We already have signed contracts between Israeli and French companies to build Dimona, with your government's explicit approval. You have no right to renege on these commitments."

"You have a point," he finally conceded. "We will do it as you say."

. . .

On November 3, 1959, at the age of thirty-six, I was elected to public office for the first time in my life. And, as intended, my work continued. By the summer of 1960, the Dimona project had moved forward apace. France was upholding its end of the agreement, and the French and Israeli workforce had broken ground on the barren plateau.

That September, I was in West Africa on orders from Ben-Gurion, as part of an effort to build stronger ties between Israel and the broader continent. I was there to attend the swearing in of the first president of the Republic of Senegal, a man who had known the inside of a Nazi concentration camp, having been taken prisoner while fighting for the French. But the trip was cut short. I received an urgent cable, ordering my immediate return to Israel. There was no indication of what the emergency entailed.

When I arrived at the airport in Tel Aviv, Isser Harel, the Mossad chief, was waiting with Golda Meir in a helicopter nearby. We barely spoke on the ride to Sde Boker, where Ben-Gurion was awaiting Harel's report.

"Explain the situation," Ben-Gurion demanded as we gathered in his sparse and humble "hut." Harel relayed two pieces of intelligence. First, Mossad had learned that the Soviets had recently flown over Dimona and photographed the construction site. Second, they received word that the Soviet foreign minister had made an unexpected visit to Washington. In his estimation, these two facts were linked—and damning. He was concerned that the Soviet government would claim that our work in Dimona was nefarious, that their foreign minister had likely demanded U.S. intervention while in Washington. Israel, it seemed, was about to be confronted by the world's only two superpowers.

"What is your recommendation?" Ben-Gurion asked of the group. Harel believed that Golda—or even better, Ben-Gurion himself—should fly to Washington at once and give assurances to the White House. Golda agreed, believing the situation to be dire, perhaps insurmountably so. I listened intently and sympathized with their concerns, but when Ben-Gurion asked me my opinion, I had to be honest.

"So what if a Soviet aircraft has overflown the Negev? What has it photographed? Just holes in the ground," I explained. We were still in the first stage of the project, an extensive excavation followed by the laying of concrete foundation. "What can be proved from that?" I asked. "After all, every building needs foundations."

As for the Soviet foreign minister, it struck me that there were a lot of possible reasons for his sudden trip to the United States, and we lacked any evidence to suggest that we were it. Besides, I argued, we weren't considering the entire chessboard. If Ben-Gurion flew to Washington and revealed the work we had undertaken, it would destroy our relations with the French.

I believed that in all likelihood, Harel's analysis was correct. But I argued that it would be a grave mistake for Israel to act prematurely. If he was right, it meant a confrontation was imminent, and I saw no reason why we needed to offer our assurances before it. Why not wait for the outcome, and offer the same assurances after the fact?

Ben-Gurion agreed with my proposal, infuriating Golda and Harel. I could understand why. They had wanted to save Israel at the last moment from what they saw as a calamity of my sole creation—and here I stood between them and Ben-Gurion, having blocked their final effort. Now there was little for them to do but wait for a possible altercation, hoping against their better instincts that they had been wrong.

On December 18, 1960, we put my theory to the test. Days earlier, newspapers around the world had published sensational reports about an unnamed small nation that was developing nuclear arms. A London newspaper soon named Israel as the state in question. On December 18 the chairman of the U.S. Atomic Energy Commission made the same case on American television. The story spread to newspapers around the world, along with spy plane photographs of the construction site.

Five days after the London newspaper first broke the story, Ben-Gurion chose to make a public announcement in the Knesset. It had become untenable to deny the existence of the program. An announcement from the Old Man was the most effective way to begin calming apprehensions.

"The reports in the media are false," he declared. "The research reactor we are now building in the Negev is being constructed under the direction of Israeli experts, and is designed only for peaceful purposes." This declaration calmed public tensions, but there was still more work to do in private. Ben-Gurion traveled to Washington for a lengthy discussion with President John F. Kennedy in the spring of 1961. He gave assurances once again that we possessed neither nuclear weapons nor evil intent, and returned to Israel confident that crisis had been averted. The work we'd begun in Dimona would continue to move forward.

Nearly two years after Ben-Gurion's visit to Washington, I found myself standing where he had: in the middle of the Oval

Office, across the desk from the president of the United States. I had traveled to Washington to conclude a deal for the purchase of antiaircraft missiles from the U.S. government. The sale represented a sea change in the relationship between the United States and Israel, and in America's willingness to support us militarily. And it had been one of the key things that Ben-Gurion raised in his meeting with President Kennedy in 1961.

Kennedy's Near East advisor, Mike Feldman, had invited me to the White House, along with our ambassador, Avraham "Abe" Harman. When I'd arrived, I was told—quite unexpectedly—that President Kennedy wanted to speak to me. He knew I was in charge of Israel's nuclear program and, according to Feldman, he had a number of questions.

Because I wasn't the head of government, it was against protocol for President Kennedy to take a formal meeting with me. Instead, I had been escorted through the side entrance of the West Wing of the White House, and around a back corridor to the Oval Office. I was meant to have bumped into President Kennedy along the way, who would then, out of courtesy, invite me to have a conversation.

Behind his desk in the Oval Office, Kennedy looked stiff and deliberate, and though he had ways of disguising it, I could tell he was coping with pain. He stood up to shake my hand, then offered me a place on the sofa. He sat adjacent to me, in a padded wooden rocking chair.

"Mr. Peres, what brings you to Washington?" he asked, in his familiar accent.

I told him that I was there to purchase the Hawk missiles, which Israel deeply appreciated. But I added that we hoped this arms agreement was just the beginning. We needed support—as much as the Americans were willing to give.

"Go talk to my brother about that," he replied, shifting attention to the matter of his greater concern. "Let's you and I talk about your nuclear facility."

Kennedy proceeded to lay out in front of me all of the intelligence the United States had gathered on the project, meticulously explaining everything his government knew, having clearly studied the findings in great detail. When he finished, it felt as though there was nothing that the Americans didn't know about the construction. And yet Kennedy knew that mystery remained, and he was preoccupied with rumors.

"You know that we follow with great concern any indication of the development of military capacity in that area," he said. "What can you tell me about this? What are your intentions as they relate to nuclear weapons, Mr. Peres?"

I hadn't expected to see the president, let alone to be asked such a question. Under the circumstances, I did my best to reassure him.

"Mr. President, I can tell you most clearly that we shall not be the first to introduce nuclear weapons to the region."

President Kennedy expressed his satisfaction upon hearing this answer, and after a few remaining pleasantries, we concluded the meeting. Once we were beyond the White House gates, our ambassador let me know his displeasure.

"What were you doing?" he demanded. "Did you get permission to say that? You just made policy in there."

"What should I have done?" I replied. "Should I have said, 'Just a minute, let me call our prime minister and make sure I word my answer correctly'? I had to make a decision, and I wasn't going to lie." When I returned to Israel I was criticized viciously by both Eshkol and Meir for the formulation of words I chose. But in time, they would adopt the phrasing as well. In fact, to my lasting surprise, my impromptu statement to President Kennedy became Israel's long-term policy. It has been described as "nuclear ambiguity," quite simply the decision to neither confirm nor deny the existence of nuclear weapons.

For nearly fifty years, nuclear ambiguity has been Israel's official position—not because the words I chose in that moment were perfect, but because the effect of them produced the structural shift in the region we'd always intended. Before destroying a state—as the Arab nations promised to do to Israel countless times in our first thirty years—a country must possess two things: first, the desire, and second, the belief that they have the military superiority to do so. The existence of Dimona may have increased our enemies' desire to destroy us. But the suspicions it generated stole from them the belief that they could overpower us.

Over time, we learned that there is tremendous power in ambiguity. By the 1970s, the conventional wisdom among leaders in the Arab world was that Israel possessed nuclear weapons. What they lacked in evidence, they filled in with rumors, which spread through the region even faster than facts. We did nothing to confirm such suspicions, and likewise nothing to dissuade them. In due time, those suspicions hardened like stone, until they were the immovable convictions of our enemies. Believing that Israel had the power to destroy them, they one by one abandoned their ambitions to destroy us. Doubt was a powerful deterrent to those who desired a second Holocaust.

Nuclear deterrence was not sufficient to prevent all wars, but it was enough to prevent a certain kind of war. In 1973, during the Yom Kippur War, Egypt and Syria caught Israel by surprise, leaving our cities vulnerable to catastrophic attack during their coordinated offensive. And yet neither country dared to attack the heart of Israel, even when they had the capability to do so; Egyptian troops were ordered not to go beyond the Mitla Pass in the Sinai, while Syrian troops stayed in the Golan Heights. After years trumpeting the destruction of Israel, Egypt and Syria had drastically narrowed their ambitions to a fight over territory lost in the previous war. Years later, Egyptian president Anwar Sadat acknowledged that he feared an attack on the cities of Israel would have justified a nuclear response.

Nuclear deterrence also created the possibility of peace. In November 1977, Sadat made his historic visit to Jerusalem, one that would culminate in a peace treaty between Egypt and Israel. Upon his arrival, the first issue he raised with President Ezer Weizman was Israel's nuclear program. And when he faced criticism from his fellow Egyptians, he described a nuclear attack as the only other possibility. "The alternative to peace is terrible," he insisted.

By the mid-1990s, Israel had made peace not just with Egypt, but with Jordan. And we were undertaking the painstaking work of forging peace with the Palestinians. In 1995, I took a trip as foreign minister to Cairo, where I met with my Egyptian counterpart, Amr Moussa. We'd come to know each other well over the years, and after a lengthy conversation, he raised an issue still clearly on his mind.

"Shimon, we are friends. Why don't you let me go have a look at Dimona? I swear I will not tell anybody."

"Amr, are you crazy?" I replied. "Suppose I shall bring you to

Dimona and you see that there is nothing there? Suppose you stop worrying? For me, this is a catastrophe. I prefer you remain suspicious. This is my deterrence."

I've told many people that I built Dimona in order to get to Oslo. Its purpose was not to fight a war, but to prevent one. It was not the reactor that mattered but the echo it generated. I had spent so much of my youth trying to secure Israel for its people. But this was a different kind of security altogether. This was the security of knowing the state would never be destroyed—a first step toward peace that started with peace of mind. In this way, I felt that our work on Dimona, an effort once marked for certain failure, had fulfilled the covenant I had made with my grandfather, but on a far grander scale: to always remain Jewish and ensure the Jewish people always remain.

CHAPTER 4

OPERATION ENTEBBE
AND THE VIRTUE
OF DARING

I have known terrorism for nearly all of my life. I wasn't yet ten years old when two Jews were murdered just beyond the edge of the forest in Vishneva. I was fifteen years old when I learned to use a rifle, not to hunt, but to guard my school from the violent uprising that terrorized our nights. I have stood at the sites of unimaginable carnage, and wept with families who lost mothers and children. Before Israel was a state, and in all the years since it became one, we have had to grow up alongside terrorism, to defend ourselves against it, to bury its victims, and to seek its solution. We have learned hard lessons through pain and tragedy—about the cost of hostility, and its causes.

The scourge of terror is not unique to Israel; it is a global crisis of increasing ferocity, one that all nations must firmly confront. It is like a deadly disease—contagious and spreading—one that cannot be defeated through compromise or concession. To give in to the demands of terrorists is to invite more and bigger demands. In dealing with terrorists, leaders would be wise to remember that when there is a gun to your head, you are not the negotiator; you are the hostage.

And yet, while the advice may be simple, it requires one of the hardest tests of leadership. Holding firm to such a position demands a willingness to make dangerous and difficult choices. It necessitates, unavoidably, the acceptance of certain risks. Modern history tells countless stories of such moments, of impossible decisions made by brave women and men on behalf of those whom they lead. Among them, there is perhaps no clearer portrait of this battle—between conviction and complexity—than the IDF operation in a place called Entebbe.

On Sunday, June 27, 1976, I entered the prime minister's office to join in the government's weekly cabinet meeting. Yitzhak Rabin was presiding. Two years earlier, Rabin and I had faced off against one another to lead the government, and in the aftermath of his victory, he had asked me to serve as Israel's defense minister. The day's meeting was much like any other: a discussion of tight budgets and tough challenges related to important work that lay ahead. None of us around the table could have known what was about to transpire as the door of the office swung open and one of my military aides stepped into the room. He hastily approached and handed me a folded-up note, scribbled in a dizzying handwriting that suggested the same urgency as his footsteps.

"Air France Flight 139 from Ben-Gurion Airport to Paris-Orly has been hijacked after a stopover in Athens," the note read. "The plane is now in the air, its destination unknown."

I passed the note to Rabin. As soon as the meeting was adjourned, he asked a smaller group of cabinet ministers to form a task force and join him in the downstairs conference room to discuss options. We shared what little we knew—which, we acknowledged, was next to nothing. It was decided that we would issue an official statement providing the initial facts as we understood them, and confirming that the government had no intention to negotiate with terrorists. Rabin adjourned the meeting, and we each began our work—to understand what had happened, and to plan for a response.

Over the coming hours, details trickled in. We learned that the terrorists who had boarded the plane in Athens were members of the infamously violent Popular Front for the Liberation of Palestine and that they had commandeered a plane with nearly 250 passengers, including more than one hundred Israelis, and twelve crew members from France. That afternoon we received a report that the plane had refueled in Libya. Mordechai "Motta" Gur, the IDF chief of the general staff, pulled me aside to say that he thought it possible the plane was headed for Israel. I phoned Rabin to describe the new intelligence. We agreed that if the hijackers did indeed want to come to Israel, we should let them. We had some experience launching hostage rescues, and doing so at our own airport on our own soil was certainly preferable if necessary. That had been the case four years earlier, when terrorists had hijacked a Sabena flight from Vienna to Tel Aviv. We were able to rescue the passengers then. But that was on our home territory. This was very different. For now, we had little choice but to wait.

In the late hours of the night, I joined Yekutiel "Kuti" Adam, chief of operations of the IDF, on a drive to the airport where the

IDF's elite commando unit, Sayeret Matkal, was rehearsing for a possible hostage rescue. I had incredible faith in the bravery and the skill of the Sayeret Matkal. They were deeply creative, strong not just in body, but in mind. They were the best fighting force in Israel. I considered them the greatest in all the world. The unit's recently appointed commander was Yonatan Netanyahu, brother of the future prime minister. I had met Yonatan a number of times, after being told by several senior officers how special he was, and how much they expected me to like him. He was a great fighter, they elaborated—astoundingly courageous—but also something of an intellectual, a lover of literature. And indeed, on the occasions when we spoke, it was just as likely that we would discuss antitank missiles as we would the poetry of Edgar Allan Poe. Born the same year as my daughter, he was young enough to be my son, but wise enough to be my contemporary.

When Kuti and I arrived, Yonatan was on a another mission in the Sinai. His deputy commander, Muki Betzer, had assumed the duty of briefing the commandos on the situation and leading their preparations for a night raid of the plane—using an empty fuselage nearby. But in the early hours of the morning, the plane changed course and was no longer headed for Israel, but for East Africa. At 4:00 A.M., we confirmed that the passenger jet had landed at Entebbe Airport, on the banks of Lake Victoria—twenty miles outside of Uganda's capital and more than two thousand miles from where we were standing.

The challenges this presented were enormous. In the aftermath of the 1973 war, Rabin and I had worked to modernize and replenish our military, and to prepare it for the "long arm" option—an ability to strike targets far beyond our immediate horizon. But no country or army had ever contemplated a challenge of this dimension. It was going to require a military operation to take place thousands of miles away, against armed terrorists and, perhaps, the Ugandan army—all carried out with suboptimal intelligence, against a ticking clock. Most of our senior military leadership seemed to feel that a military rescue operation was simply impossible.

While the challenges were great, the stakes were even greater. First, there were the hostages themselves—more than one hundred Israelis in grave danger. We would later learn that some of the terrorists were from Germany, and were barking orders in German. One of the hostages, a Holocaust survivor, had become hysterical upon hearing the language. Later she would be reminded again of the Holocaust—as would we all—when the hostages were separated into two groups, with Jews on one side and non-Jews on the other. It was a haunting whisper of the past, and a discomfiting reminder of our own obligations.

It became clear to me that we faced, fundamentally, a question of principle. If we were unable to rescue the hostages, our only alternative was to negotiate their release, ultimately giving in to the demands of terrorists. This, I feared, would create a terrible precedent with unknown consequences. "If we give in to the hijackers' demands and release terrorists," I said during one of the heated government meetings over the coming week, "everyone will understand us, but no one will respect us." Yet the opposite—however grim the results—held: "If, on the other hand, we conduct a military operation to free hostages, it is possible that no one will understand us—but everyone will respect us." I understood that attempting such an audacious and unlikely rescue posed a great risk to the passengers. But my determination to find an alternative was driven not out of lack of concern for their well-being. On the contrary, it was rooted in the interest of the lives and safety of passengers in the future. The greatest danger of all was terrorist organizations concluding that such actions as those taken in Athens were effective. One plane could become hundreds. Victims could be measured in the many thousands as opposed to hundreds.

We also risked something less measurable but equally important: our national confidence. During the 1967 war, we had demonstrated such an impressive showing of force and skill that we were seen, the world over, as tough and brave. At home, it was a powerful source of pride. After so many years of uncertainty, we came to believe that we had achieved our ultimate aim: securing a state that couldn't be undone. But in 1973, Egypt and Syria launched a coordinated assault against Israel that caught us by total surprise. We were able to fend off the attack, but at a high cost, and throughout the country there was a sudden and sharp loss in confidence. Over the course of a month we'd gone from deeply self-assured to deeply unnerved. It was a return to wariness—to openly existential questions about our security—and it created an unsettling fear that in the prideful wake of the 1967 war, the country's confidence had drifted toward arrogance. When I became defense minister the following year, I dedicated a significant portion of my work to figuring out what had gone wrong, and to correcting the deficiencies that had allowed such a catastrophe. We ordered a major overhaul of the military intelligence, which had failed to warn us of the imminent attack. In the meantime, I spent my days reading hundreds of pages of raw material, rather than relying on the Intelligence Corps's assessments. I was even known to do unannounced spot checks throughout Israel, making sure that the new rules we put in place across the military were being followed.

We were still bandaging our wounds that summer of 1976. Great empires have fallen when their people lost confidence in them. Great countries and great companies, too. Israel was fueled by the ambitions of its people, and a crisis of this nature jeopardized our own sense of self and, in turn, our future state. "If we will need to release terrorists," I wrote one night during the coming drama, "Israel will look like a rag, and even worse, she will be one."

In the face of such an extraordinary situation, I knew there was little choice but to act. When I was told there was no way to make a rescue possible, I decided to heed the words of my late mentor, Ben-Gurion, who had passed away in 1973. "If an expert says it can't be done, get another expert."

. . .

I returned home as the sun was rising on Monday morning, and phoned Rabin to brief him on the latest information we had. After a shower and a coffee, I went back to the Defense Ministry, where I spent the day, alongside dozens of others, poring over unreliable information. Intelligence was coming in from a number of sources, and much of it contradicted itself. At the end of the day, all we knew was that the plane was still on the tarmac in Entebbe. We didn't yet know the hijackers' demands.

Gur told Rabin that we had yet to come up with a solid plan, but we were looking into a possibility involving paratroopers. Rabin seemed satisfied, temporarily at least, that planning was under way, and a rescue mission remained a possibility. But that evening, after further conversation with Gur, it became clear that no one else really believed a military operation was feasible. There were too many uncertainties, they said, too many unknowns, too little intelligence, too many risks.

I shared their concerns. Even in the best of circumstances, we would need to pull off the most daring operation in our history. And these were not the best of circumstances. But I was not ready to give up.

"We have to use our imagination, and examine any idea, as crazy as it may seem," I insisted to those assembled. "I want to hear the plans you have."

"We have no plans," responded one.

"Then I want to hear the plans you don't have!" I replied.

This tug-of-war continued for several hours, but by the end of the session, we had made progress. Doubt had given way to determination among the group. Even the most skeptical among them refused to let the unlikeliness of a solution prevent them from seeking one out. This was the essential cognitive breakthrough— something I relentlessly attempted to inspire during the most challenging moments of my career. Far too often, especially under stress (and few things could have been more stressful than the Entebbe crisis), we turn inward and close down. Believing that distraction is the greatest danger, our analysis simplifies in hope of increasing not the odds of success, necessarily, but the chance we will be certain about what the outcome will be. This can be a great strategy for defense, but until one accepts that "unlikely" does not mean "impossible," the chances of developing creative solutions are severely limited.

In those tense days, I remember thinking how few armies, if

any at all, had such a group of courageous, serious people. As the discussion continued, I knew I was asking the world of them in a seemingly impossible circumstance. And yet I also knew they stood ready and willing to answer my every request, including my plea that they use their imaginations.

By the end of the session, three possible plans had emerged from the group.

The first came from Kuti Adam, who argued that if we couldn't rescue the hostages in Entebbe, we should try to get the hostages to come to us. If we could convince the hijackers to fly to Israel—perhaps in the belief that we would participate in an exchange of hostages for prisoners upon their arrival—we could conduct a raid similar to the one we'd executed so successfully with the Sabena flight.

It was a creative approach, to be sure, but it assumed we had leverage where we likely did not. Surely the terrorists had chosen Entebbe for a reason—not only because of its distance from Israel, but because they had the support of Uganda's president, Idi Amin, who we knew had greeted the terrorists as "welcomed guests." It seemed implausible that they would give up such an advantage—and surely not before having proof that we'd upheld our end of the bargain. Besides, the Sabena rescue operation had been widely publicized; it was no longer a secret playbook.

The second approach, proposed by Gur, assumed the rescue would have to take place in Entebbe. He described a scenario whereby Israeli paratroopers would sneak into Entebbe by way of Lake Victoria, launch an unexpected attack on the hijackers, and remain to protect the hostages.

This plan had the virtue of practicality, in that it described a scenario the IDF was more than capable of executing. But what it lacked, fundamentally, was an exit plan. Once the hostages were rescued, there would be no way to evacuate them. If the Ugandan army chose to respond, it could surely send a force large enough to overpower even our finest commandos.

The third approach was by far the most fantastic in terms of imagination. Major General Benny Peled, who was the commander of the Israeli Air Force, suggested that Israel conquer Uganda—or at least Entebbe itself. Israeli paratroopers would temporarily occupy the city, the airport, and the harbor, after which the hijackers would be attacked and killed. Having secured the area, the air force would land its Hercules military transport plane at Entebbe airport and use it to bring the hostages home.

On its face, the plan seemed preposterous. Gur described it as "unrealistic, nothing but a fantasy." The others agreed. And yet, of the three proposals, it was the one that had me most intrigued. Aside from its scale and ambition, it struck me that there was nothing about Peled's plan that was disqualifying. Unlike Gur's plan, this one included a strategy for evacuating the hostages. And unlike Kuti's plan, it didn't require us to manipulate the terrorists into acting against their interests. Indeed, when the meeting was over, Peled's plan was the only one I hadn't dismissed.

Late that evening, Rabin reassembled the key ministers to discuss the hijackers' demands and our options for response. We had received a list of prisoners whose release the terrorists were demanding by July 1 at 11:00 A.M. We had fewer than thirty-six hours to comply. The list included forty terrorists imprisoned in Israel, along with six in Kenya, five in Germany, one in France, and one in Switzerland. Even if I had wanted to submit to the demands, doing so would be impossible—there was not enough time to organize such a complex release across so many countries, and we had no reason to believe that the other countries would participate. The Kenyan government said that the terrorists in question were no longer in the country. The French claimed that they had already released the terrorist said to be held in their territory. The West Germans were surely not going to release the Baader-Meinhof terrorists on the list, as they had been responsible for so much horrific murder and violence.

In my view, the impossibility of the demands bolstered the argument for rescue. That is, as improbable as a military option may have appeared, it now seemed clear we were more likely to mount a successful rescue than we were a successful negotiation. In that case, I decided it was better to focus all of our efforts on mounting our best attempt. For his part, Rabin wasn't as convinced as I was about the precedent that negotiation would set. He noted that when he met with the relatives of the hostages, they reminded him that after the 1973 war, we had exchanged prisoners for the bodies of fallen soldiers. How could we now refuse to free these prisoners, when the hostages remained alive?

I understood the place of desperation the hostages' families were coming from. But, I told Rabin, we had never freed prisoners who had killed innocent civilians, and that's exactly what the terrorists were demanding. To accede to their demands would indeed set an alarming new precedent.

As the debate continued, Rabin grew impatient with me, perhaps understandably so. Though I knew that my case for a military option was both moral and practical, I was the only one in the room agitating for it. And yet I still lacked a viable, detailed plan to present to the prime minister. With less than two days before the hijackers' deadline, this made the whole exercise feel like an abstraction—and a distraction—to Rabin. By the end of the meeting, Rabin had decided that it was time for Israel to announce its willingness to release its forty prisoners. And I decided I needed a better plan.

. . .

When we first learned that the Air France flight had landed in Uganda, one of my bodyguards pulled me aside to tell me he knew Idi Amin quite well, having once served as one of his aides.

"He's going to drag this out as long as he can," he said of Amin. "He will love the attention."

As I lay awake in the early hours of Wednesday morning, I kept returning to those words. If my bodyguard was right, it meant that for very different reasons, Amin and I shared the same goal: to delay the end of the crisis. I returned to the ministry that morning increasingly convinced that Amin would ask the terrorists to postpone their deadline. In the meantime, I gathered a few IDF officers who had served in Uganda, and who knew Amin. It was a powerful moment of clarity.

The officers told me that Amin relied heavily on the judgment of those closest to him, that he loved to be in the spotlight and had great hopes of being treated as an equal on the world stage; he even imagined a day where he would win a Nobel Prize. But he was a cruel and cowardly tyrant, not worthy of his larger ambitions. One of the men recalled a time when Amin, having been handed a rifle as a gift, aimed it at the crowded courtyard of his villa and began shooting indiscriminately. They told me that Amin didn't like getting involved in other people's wars, so it was unlikely that the Ugandan army would be a major presence at Entebbe. They also told me that they didn't think the dictator would kill the hostages on his own accord: Amin had once recounted a story in which his mother warned him to never kill the Jews, that he would pay dearly for it. Still the officers made clear that he could be unpredictable. If he felt his pride was at stake, or if, as had happened in the past, he had a vivid dream during the night, there would be no accounting for his actions.

The conversation proved enormously valuable. I concluded from it that the Ugandan army didn't present a threat to a military operation, and that Amin was unlikely to support the execution of hostages while he was at the center of an international drama. I also suspected that Amin could be manipulated to our benefit—that we could appeal to his narcissism and use it to our advantage.

I asked one of the officers, Colonel Baruch "Burka" Bar-Lev, to reach out to Amin, who considered him a friend. If he was able to, I instructed him to call Amin and tell the Ugandan leader that he was speaking on behalf of the senior leadership of the government. I told Burka to play to Amin's ego—to give him the impression that Israel viewed him as a leader of great international importance—and to try to convince Amin to intervene. "Tell him he'll be blamed if something goes wrong, and it will make him look weak," I added. "Tell him he might even win the Nobel Peace Prize if he helps us."

That afternoon, Rabin convened the senior ministers to discuss the situation and review our options. He was—as were we all—

deeply concerned about the hostages, particularly the children. As a decorated former IDF commander, Rabin was well aware of our capabilities—and our limitations. He told us that whatever our official position, in the absence of a military option we would have no other choice but to negotiate.

"At this stage, I don't think a military operation is possible," he reasoned. "What do we do? Attack Uganda? How would we even reach Uganda?

"The object," he continued, "is not to act militarily, but to save people's lives. As of right now, I can't see a way to do that."

Shortly after, I convened a meeting of my own, one that Gur would coin the "Fantasy Council." My intent was to bring the most creative thinkers in the IDF together so that we could consider every known option and be bold in thinking about options that did not exist. I had asked Gur to invite those most interested in planning for the impossible. Once they arrived, I asked Gur to provide the group an update on his scheme to parachute into Lake Victoria. He had little good to report: the army confirmed that the lake was infested with crocodiles, and the previous night's rehearsal had failed. The alternative—which required speedboats—was unworkable, the Mossad chief reported, because it would require Kenya's participation, and he was certain the Kenyan government wouldn't want to risk retaliation. And there was still no clear answer for how we would evacuate the hostages once rescued.

With Gur's plan shelved, I turned to Peled. In the time between our last discussion and now, he had modified his plan to require a smaller footprint. Rather than conquer the city, Peled resolved to simply conquer the airport. He suggested dropping a thousand paratroopers from ten Hercules aircraft.

General Dan Shomron, the chief paratrooper and infantry officer, quickly raised an objection. "By the time your first paratrooper hits the ground, you won't have anybody left to rescue." The terrorists, he explained, would surely see the paratroopers falling from the sky and begin firing on the hostages.

As the conversation continued, others around the table suggested a more surgical operation—using two hundred soldiers and landing a plane at the airport instead. There was risk that the plane might be spotted by radar, but it offered an important added advantage: a way to bring the hostages home.

It was, in my estimation, the most viable plan we had, and so I asked the group to keep working through its details. The trouble was, there were still far too many things we didn't know. We were hampered by a lack of intelligence, and what we did have we couldn't necessarily trust. One report suggested that a squadron of Soviet-made fighter jets might intervene; another claimed that a full battalion of Ugandan troops had been mobilized to the airport. We didn't know how many terrorists there were, or if the hostages were even still on the plane. We were planning a rescue mission that involved our soldiers landing at the airport—with no sense of what they would find upon arrival.

After adjourning the meeting, I learned that Burka had indeed been able to speak to Amin and was anxious to debrief me. Burka had done everything that was asked of him, but Amin was adamant, claiming to be powerless to stop the terrorists on his own soil. His unwillingness to help only confirmed my view that a military rescue was our only option.

From the conversation, we were told that the hijackers had released the forty-eight non-Israeli hostages, which we later confirmed to be true. But it remained quite difficult to separate fact from fiction. Amin swore that there were thirty hijackers, though based on the manifests we thought it was closer to seven. He said that the hijackers were wearing suicide vests and had enough TNT to blow up the entire airport, which, while possible, seemed hard to believe given that they had traveled there on a commercial airline.

And yet these were the circumstances. After another sleepless night, I faced the morning feeling dreadfully dark. It was Thursday, July 1, and the ultimatum was set to expire that afternoon. And though I suspected it would be extended, I feared the carnage awaiting us if I were wrong.

Rabin scheduled an early-morning ministerial meeting. Before it began, I pulled Gur aside to discuss new intelligence we had received. Some of the forty-eight non-Israeli hostages had already reached Paris and had provided critical details. We confirmed, for example, that the hostages were being held in one of two terminals—the old terminal, we called it. They were being guarded both by terrorists and Ugandan soldiers, and they were no longer being kept in the plane. We also received detailed information on the setup of the terminal itself. To me this was sufficient to begin preparations for a rescue mission. Though I was defense minister, I knew that in order to convince Rabin, I would also need the support of others, particularly Gur. As chief of staff, he was the linchpin, without which there was no realistic path to a military option. Until I persuaded him, it made little sense to try to convince the cabinet. But he was not easily convinced.

"I, as chief of staff, cannot present this plan for the rescue of the hostages," he said after hearing the new intelligence I had shared with him. Once again, I was more or less on my own.

The ministerial committee meeting began in a sullen mood, and under a tremendous weight. With the deadline imminent, the tension was impossible to avoid. I opened the meeting by reading the transcript of Burka's phone conversations with Idi Amin. We had gotten some useful intelligence from calls, I explained, but it was also quite clear that Amin would not be the leader we needed.

The discussion turned to the passengers' families. Minister Haim Zadok informed us that the families were insisting we begin negotiations, that they expected us to do whatever was necessary to save their loved ones.

"The problem isn't simply the families' claims," I repeated for a second day in a row. "It should be made clear that negotiation and an Israeli surrender open a wide terror front in the future."

"Who is saying that this will open a terror front?" Rabin shot back.

"I am saying so."

"I request you clarify your words and elaborate further," he replied.

"Until now, the Americans have not surrendered to terror because the Israelis set the world's standard not to surrender," I explained. "If we surrender, not one country, the world over, will be able to hold. We will invite more and more of these kinds of attempts."

"This is the situation at the moment," said Rabin. "In this moment, not making a decision is itself a decision."

The debate continued for several hours, until Rabin again intervened. "I wish to clarify: We don't have time for evasions. The fundamental question is, are we willing to enter negotiations or not? I ask that government members do not avoid answering this question."

Minister Yisrael Galili responded, saying that he believed the government should begin negotiations immediately, including "showing readiness to free detainees." Rabin seconded Galili's suggestion, noting that we had made trades in the past and that he didn't want to get into a debate about why such trades, in this circumstance, were unacceptable.

"Precedents aren't the problem," I said. "The problem is the future, the people's future and the future of Israeli airplanes and aviation. We should be concerned with the fate of the people here, of what will happen to the country and its status regarding hijacking and terror, in addition to the fate of those taken hostage."

Rabin was unmoved, as I still lacked a satisfactory alternative. "I wish to know whether anyone is opposed," he said, "and I don't want any misunderstanding of the issue. I don't propose we discuss negotiations, but that the government authorizes the team to continue our attempts to release the hostages, including exchange of prisoners in Israel."

When he asked who was in favor, every person around the table raised his hand—including me. Without a clear military option to present, the thing I needed most was more time. If beginning a slow negotiation process could create delay, then perhaps we could find a sufficient window for a miracle. In the meantime, it had the advantage of keeping the lines of communication open, of my not appearing to be a pariah whose views deserved to be dismissed out of hand. If we were somehow able to present a military option, I needed credibility to gain Rabin's approval.

An hour after the meeting, Burka and Amin spoke by phone

again. Amin was insistent that Burka tune in to Radio Africa for an announcement. He wouldn't say anything else, except that he had tried and failed to intervene, and that the hostages would be killed at 2:00 P.M. as planned.

We waited anxiously for the announcement. And then, momentary relief: the hijackers had granted a three-day delay in the ultimatum. Amin was to travel to Mauritius for a meeting of the Organisation of African Unity, and the hijackers would not take any action until he returned. Suddenly, instead of hours, we had days.

I summoned Gur to my office and told him we needed to meet to discuss options. He was shocked. "You just voted with the government to surrender!" he shouted in disbelief. "It was a trick to buy time," I explained, "and now we have time. So we shall use it as best as we can." That afternoon, the "Fantasy Council" reconvened, and for the first time, it felt that a practical rescue plan was emerging. Kuti Adam and Dan Shomron had already drafted a course of action that involved landing aircraft at the Entebbe airport and then taking it over. They described it in great detail. The operation would be carried out under cover of darkness and wouldn't last for more than an hour. The first plane would land at 11:00 P.M., right in the wake of a British airliner as a way of avoiding radar detection. Out of the belly of the plane would emerge two cars that would drive toward the old terminal to unload a group of commandos who would take out the hijackers and rescue the hostages. Within ten minutes, another of our Hercules aircraft would land, out of which two more cars would emerge. Those commandos would head for the "new terminal" and take control of it, along with the runways and the fuel reservoirs. Once their missions were achieved, two more Israeli planes would land to evacuate the hostages.

We talked about every possible outcome, every variable we could think of, everything that could go wrong. The latest we could carry out the mission was Saturday night, and though there were still questions about the viability of the plan, the officers at least agreed that we had time to prepare. But Gur expressed concern. He made the case that, even if the operation worked as intended, we didn't have the ability to fly our planes all the way to Uganda without a stopover. If we couldn't get Kenya to agree to let us use their bases for refueling, the operation was simply impossible. And even if we were able to secure the consent of the Kenyan government, Gur felt we still lacked sufficient intelligence to have confidence in the operation. We still didn't even know how many terrorists we would be facing.

"Without intelligence, there is no chance I'd recommend such an operation," he exclaimed. "Some of the things I heard here aren't worthy of the IDF's general staff. If you want James Bond—you're not getting it with me!"

Mossad was working on getting us better intelligence, I told Gur. In the meantime, I asked that he authorize a task force to begin preparing for the attack; if we were able to get the intelligence we required, we had to be ready to act. Gur agreed, and appointed Dan Shomron to command the operation.

At 5:00 P.M., I met with Rabin and a small group of ministers for further discussion. To this point, I had not presented Rabin with the details of the plan we were considering. I saw only a downside in doing so prematurely. But I did continue to push for a rescue.

"If there is a military operation, it's preferable," I said. "At this point, I admit, there's no concrete proposal—only ideas and imagination. But the alternative is complete and utter surrender." My pleas were, again, largely ignored.

When the meeting was over, my confidence had fallen. Despite all the work of the people around me, despite their willingness to push hard for me and think creatively for me, I felt increasingly like I was truly alone. And though Ben-Gurion had always taught me the virtue of standing alone, I also believe that when one is all alone, he must consider whether he is the one who is wrong. I started to wonder whether my enthusiasm for the purpose had clouded my judgment about the practicality, whether I had become so committed to the principle of rescuing the hostages that I had grown blind to the reality that we could not. Now I didn't have Ben-Gurion to turn to for advice and wisdom. So I turned to the closest thing to him: my old friend Moshe Dayan.

I'd gotten word that Dayan, who was no longer in the government, was at dinner at a waterfront restaurant in Tel Aviv with guests from Australia. I drove directly to the restaurant to meet him. He was surprised to see me, as were his guests, who looked to be just starting on their soup course. I apologized and asked Dayan to step away so that we could speak briefly in private. As I started to explain the situation, a waiter came over with two glasses of red wine. I realized it was the only sustenance I'd had all day.

I described the circumstances—the daring rescue plan, the lack of intelligence, the many risks involved, the objections, the unknown consequences—and as I did I could see Dayan fill with delight.

"This is a plan that I support one hundred and fifty percent!"

he declared, dismissing the downsides as the unavoidable risks of war. "You are right to pursue this with everything you have." He reinforced my convictions at a most important time. Though I hadn't eaten, I left the restaurant fuller than when I'd arrived.

At 11:00 P.M. on Thursday, Rabin held another cabinet meeting, at which the granular details of the hostage negotiations were being discussed. I'm not sure I spoke a word. My mind wandered back to the conversation with Dayan, and forward to the persuading that still remained.

The meeting ended well after midnight, but before going home, I decided to take a run at Gur once more. We spoke for several hours—not just about the Jewish state, but about the Jewish people—about the stakes for us all. I spoke of the great danger of the military action I was endorsing, but of the greater danger that would befall all of us were we to choose surrender instead. I tried to overcome his doubts, but when we parted ways in the early hours of the morning, Gur remained unconvinced. I returned to the couch in my office and lay down for a brief respite, hoping my words might have more power with Gur as they lingered in his mind.

. . .

After what couldn't have been more than an hour or two of sleep, I woke up in sudden agony. A toothache that had been bothering me all week had gone from distracting to debilitating. And so in the middle of all the commotion, I had to excuse myself for an emergency dental appointment.

My dentist was an old friend, Dr. Langer. His son was an IDF commando, and his weekend leave had been called off. Dr. Langer surely knew why, as he had seen press reports about hostages in Entebbe. He must have wondered if an operation was about to take place, if his son was about to face mortal danger. But as he worked on my tooth, he said nothing of it—such was the man that he was.

When I returned to my office, I was bombarded with a wealth of new intelligence that had arrived while I was gone. We had sent a Sayeret Matkal officer named Amiram Levin to Paris to assist French intelligence officers with debriefing the non-Israeli hostages. One of the hostages, an older gentleman, approached Levin. "I know exactly what you need."

He told Levin that he was a former colonel in the French army and therefore knew what to pay attention to while being held in Entebbe. He drew a sketch of the so-called old terminal, where the hostages were being held, and gave a succinct description of the layout. From him we learned there were thirteen terrorists and about sixty Ugandan soldiers. He told us that the hostages were held in the main hall of the terminal, but the French crew of the plane were detained in the women's restrooms. The plane was not parked nearby. He said there was a wall of empty crates in the old terminal, which the hijackers warned were full of explosives. But there were no wires visible from the outside, nor any indication that they were being set up to explode. It was a wealth of information. Yet again, Israel found its security bolstered by the generosity of a Frenchman.

In addition to his report, we received another from Mossad. Days earlier we had approved a mission to send an aircraft to photograph Entebbe. The mission had been a success and we were now in possession of high-quality photographs of the airport. We also received confirmation from Yitzhak Hofi, the director of Mossad, that Kenya had agreed to let us use their air base for stopovers. Gur and I met in his office to discuss the new information. In an instant, his skepticism washed away. He was ready to support the plan.

With Gur's endorsement, I put everything in motion. He was to use the new intelligence to operationalize the plan with the other members of the "Fantasy Council" while I went to brief Rabin.

I walked into the prime minister's office. "At this moment," I said, "speaking personally rather than officially, I am convinced that we have a real military option available." I described the plan to Rabin, as well as the reservations among those who were working on it. I told him the whole story of the planning sessions, of the doubts raised and answered and of those still remaining. Rabin asked Hofi to join us so that he could talk through his questions.

Rabin had both political and tactical concerns. Tactically, he worried that the first plane to land might be identified and attacked before it could unload, preventing the soldiers from deploying and leaving the hostages unprotected under the care of terrorists who believed they were under assault. More broadly, he worried that the failure of such a mission could do great damage to the country. "It might do more harm to Israel than any of the other alternatives," he contended. On the tactical side, the Mossad director expressed support for the operation. Whether the risk of failure was a risk worth taking—that was a question for Rabin to answer himself.

"Anyway, I'm bound by the cabinet's decision," Rabin concluded, referring to the earlier vote to begin negotiations. He was bound, I agreed; that was true. But I asked that he give us the chance to present him with a plan. "If you support it, the cabinet can choose to support it, too."

Later that afternoon, when I convened the "Fantasy Council" in my office, Gur announced that they were ready to present a plan to the prime minister. "Walk me through the details," I asked.

While I didn't yet know what Rabin's decision would be, I knew that our success depended on being ready from the moment we were given the go-ahead. As defense minister, I was authorized to send the IDF anywhere inside Israel's borders without the prime minister's approval. So, rather than wait for an answer, I ordered the Hercules to leave the following day from Tel Aviv to Sharm el-Sheikh, in the Sinai. I knew it was the best jumping-off point for the mission—and that if we got Rabin's approval, we'd have no time to waste.

The plan was now clear. From Sharm el-Sheikh, our forces would fly through Ethiopian airspace, beyond the range of its radar capability, and approach Uganda along the same route that commercial airliners used. The commandos, led by Yoni Netanyahu, would attack the terrorists and secure the hostages in the old terminal. The other planes would follow in succession every few minutes, unloading commandos. Some were charged with taking over the new terminal, runways, and fuel stations, while others were tasked with destroying the Soviet-made fighter jets stationed nearby. Another unit would set up roadblocks on the highway, preventing reinforcements from reaching the airport in time.

Once secured, the hostages would be taken to one of the Hercules planes and take off for Nairobi for refueling. The other planes would follow behind to Kenya, and then together they would return to Israel. The operation was planned to the minute, and the commandos had already begun drilling the movements and gaming out all scenarios around the clock. They were studying maps of the airport the way their fathers and grandfathers had studied the pages of the Talmud. Still, the operation had hundreds of variables to consider, with almost countless ways that something could go wrong.

As our discussion continued, someone at the table offered a creative idea: knowing, as we did, that Amin was not in country, he proposed that we disguise one of our commandos to look like Amin, and make it appear as though the Ugandan president had arrived at the airport in his presidential motorcade. Perhaps the Ugandan soldiers guarding the old terminal would be fooled in the darkness, long enough at least to create a moment of surprise. Gur and I both loved the idea and ordered a search for a black Mercedes, similar to Amin's car, at once. Only the night before, Gur lambasted me for my fantasies of a James Bond–style mission. Clearly, he was a man transformed.

I sent a note to Rabin to share the amusing new development: "Yitzhak, final upgrade to the plan: instead of the airport's vehicle, a large Mercedes car will come out of the plane with flags—Idi Amin is returning home from Mauritius."

"I do not know if it is possible," I added, "but it's interesting."

When the meeting was concluded, we went to Rabin's office, where Gur presented the details of our plan to the prime minister and the ministerial committee. Rabin was receptive in general, but remained uncommitted. "I am still uncertain about this operation," he said. "We have never had so many hostages. We have never had such limited military information. This is going to be the riskiest operation I have ever known." He continued to pepper Gur with questions about the plan's details. "I am in favor of all the preparations going ahead, but I propose we still see this thing as subsidiary to the ongoing negotiations," he said. "If only I could get them to release the women and children . . . that would change the whole picture." He decided to convene an extraordinary government meeting the following afternoon, just before the planes would need to take off for Entebbe. Then, and only then, would we have his final decision.

That evening, Sonia and I had plans we couldn't cancel. Some weeks earlier, the Foreign Ministry had asked me to host a Columbia University professor named Zbigniew Brzezinski during his visit to Israel. The United States was in the middle of the presidential campaign, and Professor Brzezinski was expected to be named White House national security advisor should Jimmy Carter win the election. He was scheduled to come to our home that evening for the Sabbath, along with the editor of *Haaretz* newspaper and the director of military intelligence. Were we to suddenly cancel, I feared it could raise suspicions among everyone who knew about the invitation.

I left the Defense Ministry offices just before sundown and greeted Brzezinski and the others at my table. During our dinner we had a deep and fascinating discussion about global affairs, and for a time managed to avoid the hijacking. But eventually the professor brought the conversation around to Entebbe, admitting he'd been surprised that Israel was unwilling to launch a military rescue. He pressed me for an explanation. I was unwilling to lie, yet unable to tell the truth, so I spoke in vague terms about a lack of reliable information and the challenges inherent in the distance. Brzezinski seemed unconvinced, but to my relief, the conversation moved on to other topics. When the dinner was over, I kissed Sonia good night, apologized for my weeklong absence, and returned to the office straightaway.

In the early hours of Saturday, I found myself wrestling with increasingly anxious thoughts. I spent those tense waking hours imagining all of the factors that could lead to failure—both big and small. During this period, I kept a daily journal. "Who can guarantee," I wrote, "that one of these tens of thousands of items—of which the planes, the armored cars, and the weapons are built—wouldn't fail to function at the most critical moment, or at the most critical place?"

At first light, I summoned the "Fantasy Council" to my office, where I ordered them to once again review the details of the operation. "What's your report?" I asked Gur. He told me that the practice runs had gone just as planned, taking fifty-five minutes on the ground. He said that they had been unable to find a black Mercedes in all of Israel, but he assured me not to worry, as they'd found a white one of a similar model, and had already taken the liberty of painting it black.

"There is no reason not to carry out the operation," Gur announced at the end of our gathering, beaming with confidence. "The chances of success are great."

After the meeting, Gur and I rode to the airport together to bid the soldiers farewell. The team had been practicing for the most daring mission we'd ever contemplated, but even as they boarded the planes, they didn't know if it would be approved. A number of them approached me when I arrived. They wanted to know if the government was going to give them the order, and wondered if we could really be so brave. Some of the commandos came over to shake my hand and to assure me of their own confidence in the mission. I watched as they boarded the plane—Yoni in the lead, his unit by his side—and knew full well that all the bravery was theirs.

That afternoon, Rabin opened the extraordinary session of the cabinet, describing the new circumstances that had emerged. "As of today, we have a military option," he explained, before describing the contours of the operation. When he finished, I addressed the group.

"The heart-wrenching question is whether we risk the lives of innocent unarmed civilians and save the future of this country—or not. If we surrender, we encourage more operations like this," I said. "Countries around the world might understand our ways, but they will mock us in their hearts."

Next, Gur laid out the details of the plan, step by step, as well as his conclusions. The operation, as he saw it, was well calculated and calibrated, and one that he expected would succeed. He noted, of course, the possibility of casualties, but said that such risk existed "in any other operation we've ever done to rescue civilians."

"If we fail to refuel, how long is the flight?" asked one minister.

"They won't be able to return home," Gur said.

"What about weather issues over there?" asked another.

"It's risky," Gur admitted.

"What if we find out they moved the hostages' location overnight?" asked a third.

"The mission will be a complete and utter failure," said Rabin.

And yet, these were the circumstances. The mission—the first in the IDF's short history executed outside the Middle East—was unprecedented on that fact alone. Add to that the additional complexity and unknowable variables and it was, I admitted, "an IDF operation like never before." But this was the price to be paid.

At the end of a long debate, Rabin had the final word.

"I am for the operation," he announced, for the first time aloud. "I am not idealizing. On the contrary, I know what we are in for . . . The government must know that it is deciding to launch an operation where there could be a large number of casualties," he said, echoing Gur's assessment. "Nevertheless, I ask the government to approve the operation, though not with light of heart."

The decision was unanimous. Operation Entebbe was a go.

. . .

We sat in utter silence in my office, the control room of the Ministry of Defense. Rabin chewed on a cigarette. I fiddled with a pen. From the moment the planes had taken off, they had been ordered to maintain complete radio silence unless a problem arose. Now we had gathered, along with a small group of staff and advisors, to follow the operation's progress via secure radio equipment. As the planes flew over the Red Sea and into Ethiopian airspace, as they banked across Lake Victoria and prepared for their final descent, we heard nothing. The hush bred incredible tension, even as it suggested that things were proceeding as planned.

At 11:03 P.M. there was a staccato of static: the lead plane had landed safely. Then another seven minutes of silence. During that time, the cars would have exited the first plane and begun preparing to make their way in formation to the old terminal.

At 11:10 P.M., Dan Shomron's voice interrupted the quiet. "Everything is all right," he said. "Will report later."

Eight agonizing minutes later, we heard the code "Low Tide," indicating that all the planes had landed safely.

"Everything is going well," Shomron said again two minutes later. "You will soon receive a full report."

"Palestine." The code word meant the attack on the old terminal had begun.

For the next twelve minutes, we heard nothing, and our imaginations filled the void. We knew that Israeli commandos were engaged in a gunfight with terrorists and foreign forces more than two thousand miles away, but nothing more.

Finally, there was a break in the silence: "Jefferson," which signaled that the evacuation of the hostages was commencing. "Move everything to Galila," which meant they were transporting the hostages to the Hercules for boarding. We were not out of harm's way yet, but it seemed the plan was still proceeding as intended.

Then, suddenly, we heard the code words we'd been dreading: "Almond Grove," a call for medical attention to the force under Yoni's command. We heard that there were two casualties, but we didn't know the extent of the injuries. For the next few moments, we imagined the worst—that the unit had been attacked by an unexpected force, that our intelligence had been incorrect and we were only beginning to pay the price.

But just as our minds were traveling to their darkest depths, we heard the most significant code: "Mount Carmel." All the planes were in the air, the hostages safely aboard.

There was an eruption of cheers as apprehension turned to celebration. We had tried to grasp for the impossible, and now we held it in our hands. Just after midnight, Gur called me in my office to fill us in on the details on the operation.

He told us that it had taken fifty-five minutes and that all of the terrorists had been killed. We had rescued all but four of the hostages. One, Dora Bloch, had been gravely ill and, we later learned, murdered at the hospital in Uganda. The other three—Jean-Jacques Mimouni, Pasco Cohen, and Ida Borochovitch—had misunderstood the IDF soldiers' command to lie down during the firefight and had been caught tragically in the crossfire. We also confirmed that two soldiers had been wounded, but the extent of their injuries and their identities were yet unknown.

Rabin returned to his office, and I summoned Burka to my own. I wanted him to place a call to Idi Amin, one that suggested that the president had cooperated with us on the attack. It was the best way to undermine Amin's credibility with the terrorists—a chance to sever his relationship with our enemies. Burka dialed Amin's private line while I stood next to him and listened.

"President Amin speaking."

"Thank you, sir," Burka said slyly. "I want to thank you for your cooperation. Thank you very much, sir."

Amin was confused. "You know you did not succeed," he replied.

"The cooperation did not succeed?" Burka asked. "Why?"

"What has happened?" he asked frantically. "Can you tell me?"

"No, I don't know. I was asked just to thank you for your cooperation. My friends who have close connections with the government asked me to say that to you."

I called Rabin and told him about the conversation with Amin. He burst out with laughter and invited me to come down to his office to celebrate. Menachem Begin, the opposition leader and future prime minister, was with Rabin when I entered, sharing in the joy of the moment. "The Entebbe Operation," he would later say, "will heal the nation of the trauma of the Yom Kippur War." And indeed, it would.

Operation Entebbe was, in all its glory, a moment of pure inspiration in the midst of a darkening time. It sent a message to the world—about Israel's bravery, its cunning, its refusal to surrender to terrorists, and its commitment to universal values. It would come to be known as one of the most audacious operations in military history, teaching the world what those of us in the Defense Ministry already knew: that the IDF was one of the most courageous armies in the world. The warriors who had participated in the mission became heroes, celebrities at home and abroad.

It was also a critical moment of healing, returning a feeling of safety and security that had been lost in the aftermath of the Yom Kippur War. And it sent a message to Jewish people all over the world, that the nation had a state that could protect them.

Rabin and I decided that we would release a simple statement to the press, which we drafted together. It was only one sentence long. "IDF forces have tonight rescued the hostages and aircrew from Entebbe Airport."

By three o'clock in the morning on July 4, I returned to my office and, at last, planted myself on the couch, ready to catch the first sleep I'd had in days. But despite my exhaustion, I lay there restlessly, imagining the hostages in the belly of the Hercules—what they must have been thinking and feeling. When I closed my eyes, I thought about the extraordinary fearlessness of the IDF, as well as the members of the "Fantasy Council," men who had exercised every ounce of creativity to develop the plans, even when they were certain my optimism was misplaced. Still, they never dismissed the importance—and possibility—of a mission. Without people of such character, no rescue would have ever been mounted.

I heard a rustle at the door, and opened my eyes to see Gur standing in front of me. The last time I saw him he was smiling and cheering. Now his face was sullen and sunken. It was the face of a man who had learned something tragic, but couldn't find the words to share it.

"What is it?" I asked, as I got to my feet.

"Shimon," he said meekly, "Yoni's gone. He was struck by a bullet from a sniper in the control tower. It pierced his heart."

I turned away from Gur and faced the wall. In all of the tension of the week, I had steeled myself, holding my emotions tightly in place. I had no words for Gur, nor did he have any more for me. Instead, he left my office and I burst into tears.

The next morning, Rabin and I went to the airfield to greet the rescued hostages and the returning commandoes, who had been led by Muki Betzer after Yoni's death. There was such relief in the eyes of the passengers, who had spent so much time in the depths of terror, with no way of knowing we were coming to save them. Their grace and gratitude were so meaningful, such a poignant reminder of the operation's human dimension. I watched as families reunited—children embracing their mothers, husbands held tight by their wives. I witnessed such beautiful moments, as incomprehensible worry turned into uninhibited joy. And yet, within, I was stricken with sadness. Yoni's loss was a reminder of the operation's human dimension, too.

"What burdens didn't we load on Yoni's and his comrades' shoulders?" I would say the next day in my eulogy for our fallen hero. "The most dangerous of the IDF's tasks and the most daring of its operations; the actions that were farthest from home and the closest to the enemy; the darkness of night and the solitude of the fighter; the taking of risks, over and over again, in times of peace and in times of war.

"Yonatan was a commander of valor. . . . He overcame his enemies by his courage. He conquered his friends' hearts by the wisdom of his own heart. He didn't fear danger and victories didn't make him vain. . . . By falling he caused an entire nation to raise her head high."

. . .

What did you consider when you made your decision regarding Entebbe?"

In the forty years since the operation, I have been asked that question in many ways by many people. But never was it more poignant than on April 24, 1980, when it was asked of me in the White House by President Jimmy Carter.

I had been in Washington that week, then a leader of the Israeli opposition. President Carter's office had scheduled an early-morning meeting with me. When I arrived, the secretary of state and the vice president accompanied me to the Oval Office, but Carter asked for them to wait outside.

It had been about 170 days since a group of Iranian students stormed the American embassy in Tehran and took American diplomats and staff workers hostage. President Carter had asked his national security advisor—and my former dinner companion—Zbigniew Brzezinski to develop a hostage rescue plan. After repeated failed attempts at negotiation with the Iranians, Carter was preparing for military action.

"What would you do, Mr. Peres?" he asked. "What did you consider with regard to Entebbe?"

I told him that if there was a realistic possibility of a military option, I would take it. Our problem was that we had so little information, we were forced to work in the dark. But even when we got the information we needed, there was still a great risk. But this is true of every operation, I said. So in the end, we decided to take the chance, and we found virtue in risk.

President Carter thanked me for my advice and we parted ways. What I didn't yet know, but would soon learn, was that he had already launched a daring mission earlier that morning. Having stared down the same barrel, he had made the same choice. But unlike Operation Entebbe, the results were disastrous. Some of the helicopters suffered technical failures, with one crashing into their Hercules, killing eight troops and forcing the mission to be aborted. It was a terrible tragedy.

The next afternoon, I received a call from Barbara Walters, the well-known American news anchor. "Have you heard the news?" she asked.

"Surely, I heard the news. Everybody heard the news," I acknowledged.

"What's your opinion about it?"

"I think President Carter made the right decision. If a helicopter hits an airplane, what can you do? You cannot be a president and a soldier at the same time. I think he was courageous, and it's unfortunate that the operation failed. But this is a risk you have in every operation."

That, in its simplest terms, is what I fundamentally believe. It is only after we see failure that we can know if we misjudged the risk. Of course historians will compare Operation Entebbe's success and Carter's failed attempt. But one must also avoid the temptation to overlearn specific tactical lessons born out of failure or success. I believe that the decision to mount a rescue in Uganda was the right one. Had it failed, the decision would still have been correct. This is one of the hardest things for some leaders to understand: a decision can be right even if it leads to failure. That isn't to suggest that the American hostage rescue failed simply as a matter of bad luck. Militaries must do the extensive preparation and planning required to execute such a complicated mission. But while it is possible—and important—to mitigate the likelihood of failure, leaders cannot do away with risk entirely. In 2011, the careful planning of President Barack Obama's raid against Osama bin Laden's compound in Pakistan did not prevent one of the U.S. helicopters from falling out of the sky. The operation succeeded anyway, almost miraculously, and in so doing earned its place beside Entebbe. But it is wrong to let the success of the mission come to define the courage of the president's decision. After all, he had to summon that courage before the outcome could be known.

Given the thin line between success and failure, knowing that what works in one circumstance might be disastrous in another, what do such operations have to teach us? It's certainly not that daring military action is or isn't the better course; it's that daring thinking about one's options is *always* the better course.

History hinges on successes and failures. But reaching for the former to avoid the latter does not depend on our capacity to hope. It depends on our capacity to think clearly, to choose wisely, and ultimately, to make the moral choice—even in the face of danger. The "Fantasy Council" succeeded because it established an arena for tireless curiosity and radical suggestion. If leaders demand allegiance without encouraging creativity and outside inspiration, the odds of failure vastly increase. This is one of the great lessons of Entebbe, but it is enveloped in an even larger one: without emboldening people to envisage the unlikely, we increase risk rather than diminish it.

CHAPTER 5

BUILDING THE
START-UP NATION

The early Jewish pioneers arrived in the land of Israel with nothing, only to find a place that offered almost nothing in return. They found that the land—mostly a disobliging, stony soil—was unusually challenging for growing food. Half of it, the Negev, in the south, was desert. Water shortages were so chronic that they dried up the beds of the Jordan River and threatened to empty the Sea of Galilee. The more fertile north was plagued by malaria. It was a holy place, but they would find it was not an oily place—one of the few stretches of land in the region without deposits of petroleum. The early pioneers faced a staggering challenge without expertise or experience. The ending of their story wasn't fated to be happy.

And yet today, nearly seventy years after the founding of the state, Israel is not a hopeless desert of permanent poverty—it is a technological miracle, a hub of scientific enterprise that is envied by the great economies of the world. In a country with a little more than eight million people, we have become home to more than six thousand start-ups, the highest density found anywhere in the world.

How did this happen? How did we start up a nation from nothing and transform it into a nation of start-ups? The answer lies in a paradox: having nothing was at once our greatest challenge and our greatest blessing of all. Without natural resources, our hopes were tied to our own creativity. The choice the pioneers faced was stark: succeed or starve. Indeed, the decision to move forward—despite the sheer improbability of success—was not an elective one; it was a matter of necessity. As precarious as our fate in Israel may have seemed, it remained what it always was: our best and only true hope.

So they fought. They planted fields and groves, and beat the desert back into retreat. They dug wells in the sand. When the soil failed to produce and they went to bed hungry, they vowed to find a solution. They started a research institute in 1921, where they could study seeds and soil and irrigation and livestock, where they could search for new ways to eke better crops from the land. Findings made their way to the kibbutzim right away, where they could be put into practice, improved, and refined.

Much of the efforts were focused on mere subsistence. To battle the food shortage, researchers developed seeds and planted crops that could last longer in storage—which is how the cherry tomato got its start. To battle the water shortage, they developed new recycling techniques, until nearly half of their crops were grown with water already once used. They invented a process called drip irrigation, which could water a field with up to 70 percent less water without harming the crops. At the time, they didn't imagine that it would become one of the world's most important agricultural innovations, that it would be exported and replicated to help feed the whole world. They simply knew that we were depending on them, that their work was feeding our families while serving our cause.

It was this same spirit that waves of new immigrants brought with them when they returned to the homeland. They had arrived in Israel having lost nearly everything: their homes, their communities, their families, their whole way of life. Returning home to Israel was not merely an act of desperation, but one of courage and bravery. It meant fighting through chaos, traveling great distances under a cloud of uncertainty. They arrived with little by way of possessions, but with a sense of confidence and a daring spirit, a focus not on what they lost, but on what they might gain. They rejected hierarchy openly and assertively, as though the chutzpah of Israel was already hardwired into their DNA. They also brought skills and experience and ingenuity. In the late 1980s, for example, Soviet Jews made up only 2 percent of the Soviet population, but by one estimate, made up 20 percent of its engineers and 30 percent of its doctors. So, when Soviet leader Mikhail Gorbachev finally opened his borders in 1989, more than a million Jews immigrated to Israel, tens of thousands of whom were brimming with expertise and a yearning to build something new. At every stage of our development, from the era of the pioneers to the era of the entrepreneurs, immigration replenished our communities and helped us imagine anew.

I was once asked by the founder of a young start-up what I thought was the most important lesson I'd learned about innovation through the years. "It is a complicated question," I admitted, "but I will give you a simple answer. Israel was born so Jews could finally cultivate their land with their own hands. But the most important thing to remember is that we depended more upon our brain than our muscle. We learned that the treasures hidden in ourselves are far greater than anything that can be found in the ground."

It was a lesson I learned again and again. At Ben-Shemen we didn't just learn how to till the fields; we learned new methods being developed in real time to yield more fruits from our efforts. At Alumot, the work of cultivating continued, but the learning never ceased. There were new and hopeful discoveries happening all the time, which we shared from kibbutz to kibbutz, and practiced until we reached mastery.

I had come to see innovation not only as a tool to solve problems but as an animating principle that required its own way of thinking. And so, as we worked to build the IDF, I kept one eye on the present crisis, and one toward the horizon. I knew that it was not just arms and alliances that we required, but scientific breakthroughs—the comparative advantages that could help us defend ourselves from the armies aligned against us.

It was this sense, that we could build something out of nothing—and that our future depended on it—that drove me to build an aviation industry in Israel. It's what drove me to build the nuclear facility in Dimona, at a time when the country couldn't yet feed itself. I couldn't have known that from our early efforts to repair airplanes we would become a world leader in satellites and unmanned aerial vehicles, even send an Israeli astronaut, Ilan Ramon, into orbit. When I established RAFAEL, a weapons development program, I couldn't have known that it would one day give us the protection of an Iron Dome. But what I did know is that we were laying a foundation for the future. What I did know is that by training thousands of scientists—in manufacturing and mechanical engineering; in particle physics and molecular sciences—we were cultivating knowledge, the most powerful tool for shaping the future.

Of course, there were sometimes skeptics, and not just of projects as ambitious as Dimona. When I was deputy defense minister, I spent a huge amount of my time trying to figure out what new technology could give us a comparative advantage. When I wasn't in my office, I was often visiting Israel's research institutions and universities, meeting with professors and practitioners, absorbing their work. In 1963, there was a buzz of excitement about an Israeli-designed computer that was being used at the Weizmann Institute. I was eager to see them in operation. What I found was extraordinary—a masterpiece of machinery that required a team to manage. This is what the army needs, I thought—one computer could replace one thousand soldiers and give us more data than they alone could gather. I spent many days and nights with the group that managed the computer, learning how it worked, and how it might work on behalf of the military. I returned to the ministry thoroughly convinced of its value, insisting that we purchase one of our own.

"Where are you going to put it?" one general said incredulously of the enormous machine.

"What would we do with it?" another asked. "Can you take a computer with a division into the field? Of course you can't! We don't even have enough tanks, and you're talking about computers. A tank shoots. It fires. What on earth can a computer do?"

As I had already learned by then, even the brave and the bold can fall victim to pessimism. But it didn't take long before the creative spirit of their fellow Israelis proved them wrong. We learned to use computers, first, to improve our battle readiness, but soon to develop advanced weapon systems. Technology built for one purpose often profoundly served others. The weapon systems' technology would later be used in a medical imaging device that has saved lives all over the world.

By 1974, Intel, one of the world's largest technology companies, chose Israel as a site for research and development, as we began earning a global reputation for talent and tenacity. But despite our potential, there was nothing inevitable about the path that led us to "Silicon Wadi"—quite the opposite. By the early 1980s, the old economic order under which we had organized started to collapse. I would soon have to confront one of the greatest challenges of my life and one of the greatest threats Israel had ever faced.

. . .

Thinking back on the frightful days of the economic crisis, I am reminded that while people tend to be pessimistic, history is optimistic.

It was September 1984, in the waning days of summer, that I took my seat in the Old Man's chair as prime minister of the State of Israel. The right-wing parties, led by the Likud, had been in power for seven years when the 1984 elections were held. In that time period, Israel had faced an increasingly deteriorating economic and security situation, and voters were eager for change. The Likud party bore the brunt of the backlash, losing seven seats. But the Ma'arach Party (the Labor Alignment that preceded the

Labor Party) was not the beneficiary; a number of smaller parties were. As a result, the Ma'arach ended up with forty-four seats, only three more than the Likud. With the minor parties unwilling to join a coalition, we were left with only one way to form a governing majority: a unity government between Labor and Likud. Yitzhak Shamir and I negotiated an agreement that involved a rotation of leadership: For the first half of the four-year Knesset term, I would serve as prime minister and Shamir as foreign minister. At the conclusion of that period, we would switch positions. It was not the outcome I had hoped for, but there was no time for disappointment. My truncated tenure became its own call to action, demanding the most efficient and intensive period of work we could possibly muster.

I had an aggressive agenda: to withdraw our forces from Lebanon and to begin peace negotiations with Jordan and the Palestinians. But I had not taken office in a vacuum. I had done so during an economic collapse so severe, it threatened to destroy our state from within. On the day I took office, the annual inflation rate in Israel had reached a horrific 400 percent. After more than ten years of economic dysfunction, the shekel was on its way to becoming worthless. Tens of thousands of Israelis had already been left in financial ruin by the crisis and millions more were expected to follow. Grocery store clerks would go down the aisles, often once a day, stamping new price tags on goods as the value of the shekel continued to plummet. People began hoarding their phone tokens because they weren't based on the shekel and didn't lose value. There was a well-worn dark joke, told with a sense of foreboding, that it was cheaper for Israelis to take taxis than buses because you could pay for a taxi at the end of the ride.

Israel's economy had not always been this way. Between 1948 and 1970, gross domestic product per capita nearly quadrupled, even as the population tripled in size. This was the result of massive government investments intended to build the state's foundation, from housing to roads to electrical grids and ports. But in the 1970s, things began to change. Fending off the attack of the Yom Kippur War had required the military to call up thousands of reservists, temporarily disrupting the private sector. After the war, Israel increased its defense budget dramatically. That spending, along with a major new social program, created an enormous budget deficit. At the same time, Arab members of the Organization of the Petroleum Exporting Countries (OPEC) imposed an oil embargo on countries that had come to Israel's aid during the Yom Kippur War, which created a global recession. The combination caused growth to slow, and then to cease, which led in turn to inflation. The cost of government-subsidized social programs increased, and with it, so did the deficit, worsening inflation considerably. Seemingly all at once, we were spiraling uncontrollably toward economic disaster.

At the time, our economy was organized far differently than it is today. It was a socialist system, one where the government played a role in nearly every aspect of economic life. It was the creator of industries, as well as their owner. It was the arbiter of economic and monetary policy, and dismissive of market forces, generally. That said, there were some sectors where the economy was mixed. The banks, for example, were privately owned, as were many businesses. We created the system to be uniquely Israeli, with the expectation that we could build an economy based on shared values and not simply supply and demand. But as commerce became more global and companies became multinational, we learned that there were limits to what we could control. The actions the government had undertaken to shield the population from the brunt of the slowdown—raising taxes on businesses to prop up salaries—were having the opposite effect. Instead of fending off the beast, they fed it, creating an inflationary spiral that would devastate the country. By 1979, inflation had risen to 111 percent. Within a decade, the floorboards of the economy began to buckle under the pressure. In 1983, the Tel Aviv Stock Exchange crashed, and four out of Israel's five banks had to be nationalized to prevent them from failing.

The high-tech industry was not fully immune to these forces, but it remained resilient even as the rest of the economy began to collapse. The industry was export oriented, which meant its products were largely purchased in dollars. Its public companies did not trade on the Tel Aviv Stock Exchange. And despite the rising price of oil, the industry was producing software and miniaturized hardware, which could be delivered without concern for high shipping costs. Products were delivered on time, development projects carried out. In later years, one of the sector's big selling points to investors was that, even in such dire times, it had always delivered.

But while the tech sector continued its forward motion, the rest of the economy came to a standstill. Economic pain sparked economic panic, and it seemed every day there were angry demonstrations and protests.

During my campaign for prime minister, I had asked a group of economic experts—Yoram Ben-Porath, Amnon Neubach, Michael Bruno, Eitan Berglas, Emmanuel Sharon, and Haim Ben-Shahar—to work on a plan to help stanch the bleeding. I was no expert in economics, but I knew that if I sought trusted advice and studied thoroughly, I could build the fluency I'd need if I were to prevail in the election. I had certainly done it before.

When I received their proposal, it was made immediately clear to me that I didn't just face an economic challenge, but also a leadership challenge. The only road back to a stable economy would necessarily require pain, distributed across the entire economy, though not equally. I was thrust into the center of a web of competing interests: trade unionists, who rightfully feared the consequences for Israel's workers; employers, who feared that a Labor prime minister would pass the burden to them; and my ministerial colleagues, who were in favor of cutting government spending—so long as the cuts didn't come from their own budgets.

Though the details of a plan had yet to be determined, I knew with certainty that the deal I would be negotiating could not be incremental or piecemeal; nor could it come around after years of debate. It would have to be sweeping, dramatic, and swift—a structural transformation—indeed, an economic revolution. What we required was the kind of reform that is nearly impossible to pass, especially in the middle of a deeply uncertain political climate, with a country already suffering the devastating effects of a crisis.

The path was so fraught that I had friends urging me to decline the prime ministership, out of fear that I would shoulder the blame for a calamity I had not caused and could not solve. "Let Shamir own the consequences," they urged. These friends meant well, but I had never been one to believe that the best course of action was to retreat from risk. And so I accepted the challenge, knowing I was being asked to perform major surgery with limited anesthetic.

As soon as I took office, I asked my economic team to provide a full briefing on the status of the plan. Though there was some disagreement among them about the more technical details, there was broad agreement about the approach. But consensus didn't mean they weren't concerned. One of their primary worries was that any major structural reform could send a shock through the system that would provoke foreign investment to flee the country. Such an outflow would undermine any plan we put in place, no matter how comprehensive. The only solution, my team explained, was to get a commitment from the United States (by then having succeeded France as our most important ally) to provide an umbrella loan—a guarantee of foreign assistance as a backstop for a worst-case scenario. I told them to continue refining policy options for me with the assumption that I could secure the loan, then had my staff begin immediate preparations for a trip to Washington, D.C.

Shortly after taking office, I was greeting Secretary of State George Shultz at the State Department. I was escorted into a meeting with Herb Stein, a well-respected former White House economic advisor, who, at Shultz's direction, had spent more than a year working on solutions to the Israeli crisis. Stanley Fischer, a monetary policy expert from the Massachusetts Institute of Technology, was also a lead part of the effort, though he was unable to attend this first meeting. I thanked Shultz and Stein, agreeing we required swift action and informing them of the plan our own experts were ready to deploy. The Israeli economists had estimated that we would need a loan of $1.5 billion as part of the stabilization plan we sought to pursue. So naturally, when the discussion turned to the issue, I started by asking for $4 billion.

Stein listened closely but was noncommittal. Before agreeing to provide the loan, he and Fischer would want to help shape the details of our reform package. I agreed that this was essential, and proposed that we set up a task force between the United States and Israel, much in the way we would approach a joint military operation, with our best economists in place of generals. This struck me as the best way to build America's confidence in our efforts—and it had the benefit of giving us access to more expertise.

I returned home after the meetings in Washington to manage the most challenging aspect of the crisis: getting the workers and employers to agree with—and participate in—the implementation of the plan. This was not something that could be managed through a political coalition alone; it required an economic coalition. I convened the leaders of the Histadrut trade union (which was both a more traditional union and, in concert with Israel's long-standing socialist orientation, the owner of some of the country's largest business enterprises) together with the Employers' Association, the government's most senior economists, and the minister of finance, Yitzhak Modai. The first meetings were tense. The room overflowed with objection as the government officials briefed the attendees on the plans we were considering. None of the parties were willing to accept the inescapable reality: that for the economy to survive, sacrifice would be required by all, and the cost would be severe. When I explained that the subsidies we'd been providing to prop up salaries and control the prices of basic staple foods were actually causing more economic pain than they were alleviating, the trade unionists became animated with anger.

"This is madness," I recall one of them saying. "The economy is collapsing and you want to pull the rug out from under the workers? I never imagined I'd hear a Labor prime minister propose something so terribly draconian." It was an understandable reaction. I, too, had never imagined myself in a position where I would need to pull back on the safety net I so strongly believed in. But I knew that without such cuts, hyperinflation would continue to ravage the lives of those very same workers, and in increasingly worse ways, with no end in sight.

The exchange was similarly intense with the Employers' Association when we discussed the need for a nationwide freeze on prices. "That will drive us out of business!" one exclaimed. "You're talking about saving the economy, but an action like that would destroy it!" Again I sympathized with their concerns, but here, too, I knew that failing to take such measures would lead to an economic situation that few businesses could survive.

Regular meetings with Histadrut, the Employers' Association, and our economics team continued over the coming months. I wanted to be sure that they were fully briefed on our efforts, that they had a clear and constant understanding of the crisis, with the hope that they would eventually come to the same conclusion I had. I also wanted to be sure that they felt that their concerns were heard, to see me as a trusted broker, someone with their interests—and the country's—at the very front of my mind. During the course of the negotiations I put forth a number of temporary package deals to address the most urgent concerns around the table. These deals were meant to provide us with the time—and a bridge to the more dramatic structural reforms—that we would need. But they were little more than half measures, and the relief they provided was both minimal and fleeting.

What became clear over time was that there was a path forward to an agreement—one that was conditioned on the very trust I was seeking to develop. Neither the employers nor the unions believed the government would have the courage to make its own major sacrifice—a dramatic decrease in spending across every ministry and department. They had heard the speeches of my ministerial colleagues decrying the consequences of hyperinflation, but they expected strong resistance when it came time to enact cuts to their own ministerial budgets. I realized that if the government couldn't prove its own commitment to making hard and painful choices, we could never expect the unions and employers to do the same. We would need to act first.

In between these trust-building sessions, I had returned to Washington to meet again with the American and Israeli economic teams, and to get assurances that we would receive the loan that our stabilization effort required. The response from Fischer was generally positive, but it, too, was conditional. He handed me a typed list—ten structural and budgetary reforms quite drastic in nature—and told me that the loan was contingent upon Israel enacting every last one.

I read over the list, took several minutes to consider it, then handed it back to Fischer.

"Okay," I said calmly. "We will accept all of these conditions."

The gentlemen in the room seemed stunned, having expected me to object and to negotiate aggressively, as is my nature. Yet my reasoning for accepting the terms was actually quite simple. Stanley Fischer is a brilliant economist, and I was in no position to argue with him on the merits of the costs and benefits of each demand he had made. I also trusted the American team. They had no incentive to add superfluous conditions to their list. And most of what was included was already a part of the plan the Israeli team had produced. There was a strategic consideration as well: by placing this pressure on me, the United States was actually alleviating some of the pressure at home. That is, I calculated that the plan was more likely to be palatable in my negotiations with business and labor if it were seen not as an Israeli proposal, but as an American demand that we would have to meet in order to secure the guarantee that both business and labor knew was required.

I returned to Jerusalem and convened our team of economists at my home in the first week of June 1985. I wanted to brief them on my conversation with Fischer, and to discuss the worsening situation. The ensuing discussion lasted well into the early morning, finally coalescing around a basic set of principles. When the meeting finally concluded, I instructed the attendees to form a small working group that could turn our conversation into an actionable plan.

"I intend to bring a plan to the cabinet at the end of the month," I announced. "There is no time to waste."

Over the course of the following three weeks, our working group would meet for marathon sessions, finalizing the terms of the plan and refining them into the precise technical language that would become law. In the end, we had polished and perfected a dramatic stabilization program. First we would devalue the shekel, slash $750 million in government subsidies for basic commodities, and order a temporary freeze on wage increases. This, we expected, would result in a steep rise in prices, which we would counter with an eventual across-the-board price freeze. Second, we would implement a substantial round of spending cuts across every government ministry. Third, we would introduce a new, more restrictive monetary policy to prevent such inflation from happening again. It was dramatic in its scope and its reach—and though there was a great deal of anxiety about whether it would work, we believed we'd struck the right balance. We were hopeful about its prospects for success.

The working group formally submitted our proposal to me on Friday morning, June 28. I thanked them for the outstanding— indeed, backbreaking—effort, and for their tireless service to country.

"I intend to present the plan to the cabinet on Sunday," I told them, "and I promise you, I will not accept anything short of full approval."

The extraordinary cabinet session began under the highest of tensions. Before approving the plan, we would have to identify hundreds of millions of dollars in spending cuts. I vowed to wield the knife myself, personally reviewing every item in the budget greater than $100,000, making even the most minor of expenditures a subject of discussion. In this I would both ensure that we were going far enough and shield others in the cabinet from some of the criticism that might result.

As for the stabilization plan itself, it appeared we would have a majority. Modai, having been cooperative and helpful in the effort to craft the plan, was supportive of it, as were Foreign Minister Shamir and Transportation Minister Haim Corfu. If I could hold them through the budget-cutting process, it seemed likely to prevail. But the remaining ministers, skeptical of the plan's chances for success, preferred to continue giving speeches about the crisis rather than take a controversial vote and ownership of its outcome. They vowed instead to filibuster the session in order to prevent a vote from happening—ostensibly killing the plan. In their obstinacy, they didn't appreciate how willing I was to fight. "Gentlemen, we are going in for a long session. Tomorrow morning, we will have an economic plan," I commanded, "or I will resign and there will be no government."

One by one, I worked my way through each ministry's budget, calling out programs to be cut. When someone objected, I countered by guiding the discontented party through the plan's fine print. I let everyone speak, no matter how long or ill-intended their remarks. The sessions continued through the night and into the early hours of the morning. Some ministers complained of exhaustion. I dismissed the complaints. "An Israeli minister shouldn't sleep," I told them. "During the war we debated for entire nights; it is a minister's duty to stay awake." Not everyone listened. There was even a point when we were making cuts to a particular ministry budget, only to realize that its minister had dozed off. He was snoring.

By dawn, the budget cutting was complete, and it was clear I had a majority of ministers in support of the program. What was left was only to wait out the filibuster, to prove to the weakening opposition that I would not end the session without a vote. Finally, twenty-four hours after it had begun, the opposition gave up on the filibuster and I was able to call a vote. Fifteen ministers voted to approve the plan, while seven opposed it and three abstained.

I left the session feeling a sense of accomplishment, but also a wary apprehension. Despite all of my assurance (and reassurance) during the back-and-forth with my opponents, I couldn't be sure that the program would work, and I was fearful that we lacked other options if it failed. I also wondered if the government's willingness to share in the sacrifice would be sufficient to bring the unions around to embracing the plan.

I would soon have my answer. On the morning of July 1, 1985, we released a statement describing the program we had just approved. I prepared a speech for delivery later that day, knowing that the Israeli people would want to hear from their prime minister, that they would need to understand what we had done—and why—and how it was going to lead them out of the darkness. I arrived that afternoon at the television station, where I reviewed my remarks once more before taking a seat behind the desk and in front of the camera, ready to broadcast live to the country. But before I could speak, the studio technicians stood up in unison and walked off the set.

One of my advisors hurried over to explain. "What is the meaning of this?" I asked, frustrated at the confusion, and the lack of respect being paid to the office. "The Histadrut has gone on strike," she told me. "They made a call. Told everyone to leave. They don't want the people to hear what you have to say."

I put my frustrations aside, in recognition of the critical work that still needed to be done. Without the cooperation of the Histadrut, the stabilization plan was doomed to fail. I needed to persuade them to relent.

We would spend the next two weeks negotiating. I worked to show them, as honestly and openly as I could, that as painful as the program would be in the short term, it was the only option to save the Israeli economy for our children. They begged me to find ways to compensate workers so that we could curb the economic shock, and I was forced to remind them, again and again, that doing so would only restart inflation's deadly spiral. In the end, we came to an agreement: the unions agreed to suspend the strike and reluctantly embrace the program, and I promised that as soon as the economy stabilized, I would do all I could to help raise living standards again.

It took less than a month to see the fruits of our labor. In August 1985, inflation fell to a stunning 2.5 percent. By the end of the year, it had stabilized at 1.5 percent, and it continued to decline over time. The unemployment rate had ticked up by a little more than 1 percent, which was far less than the big jump we had feared. Eventually the plan would be hailed around the globe, becoming the subject of papers and lectures at the finest universities—a new and novel approach to a dark and difficult crisis that could be replicated throughout the world.

. . .

The speed of the healing gave me the room to breathe and to think about the critical next steps we would take as a state. We had rescued the economy, but in a sense we were saying goodbye to it, too. The socialist framework of our founding was no longer viable. We had to take our first steps toward capitalism—to embrace and then master a private-market approach. And yet despite starting anew, we weren't starting from nothing—far from it. We had a strong high-tech industry supported by extraordinary universities and research institutions. We had one of the most highly educated populations in the world, among them thousands of engineers with great talent and ambition. We had mandatory service in the IDF, where young men and women learned that questions are as important as orders, and that no title or rank can absolve someone from explaining his or her intentions and goals. And of course, we had our culture of chutzpah, a well-earned reputation as a nation of risk takers.

What we needed now was to cultivate these advantages in the private sector. We needed entrepreneurs ready to turn their ideas into start-ups; venture capitalists to invest in their ideas, while providing support and guidance; and multinational technology companies to use Israel as a critical hub, providing our workers with training and supply chains and partnerships.

First, we would have to free our engineers from their roles in government, creating the pool from which start-ups could hire, and giving the visionaries the chance to build something of their own. That work began in a way few would have expected—with a decision I made to kill a project I had nurtured from infancy, one I'd long considered a bold and noble dream.

After the Six-Day War, France, which had been our principal military supplier, had turned its back on us. Charles de Gaulle, who had championed the Israeli-French relationship in the past, had suddenly found us to be an obstacle in his broader strategy. Having dedicated himself to improving relations with the Arab world, de Gaulle used the war in 1967 as reason to impose a temporary arms embargo in Israel, and in so doing, prove his commitment to his new trading partners. At the same time, Great Britain backed out of an agreement to sell tanks to Israel. We had no immediate way to replace our damaged fighter jets, no spare parts for the ones still in working order, and no sure way to replenish or supply frontline battle equipment. The United States had stepped up to fill the gap, but gave us cause for concern during the subsequent Yom Kippur War, when the replenishments they offered were inexplicably delayed. It had become clear that by relying on foreign governments for security assistance, we could also be held hostage to the changing tides of foreign politics.

When I became defense minister in 1974, resolving this dilemma was one of my highest priorities. I believed it was time for Israel to make an investment in our own military machinery several times greater than anything we had done. In 1980, we announced the centerpiece of that program—a long-range strike fighter known as the Lavi, which means "lion" in Hebrew. The jet was designed to be incredibly versatile, capable of traveling at high speeds over great distances with heavy payloads, and operated using the most advanced software systems of the day. The Lavi program seemed to capture the imagination of the Israeli people almost instantly, seen as a shining example of our boldness, a proof point that a nation as small as ours could still compete with the world's greatest economic powers.

But it wasn't to be. The Lavi would become a victim of the economic collapse, and an anachronism for the new economic order. Stabilizing the economy had required, among other things, a massive cut to defense spending. Despite having the technical prowess to manufacture the plane, we no longer had the budget to dedicate to its development. Ending the project would be personally difficult, the jet having taken flight so many times in my imagination. But out of the failure, I could recognize opportunity. The Lavi project represented the economy of the past—a top-down, government-run operation. By canceling it we would send a crucial signal to world markets about the seriousness of our transformation, while creating a flood of newly available experts who would populate private companies and start up new ones. When I introduced the bill to kill the project there was a heated debate, and great shock that it was me, of all people, calling for the end of the program. But I knew I was doing the right thing. When the Lavi project was officially canceled, the deciding vote was mine.

Next, we would need to build a venture capital system. Venture capital firms provided more than just funding; they provided guidance on how to manage a company, how to grow it at scale and at speed, and how to market products to the world. While Israel had a long history of developing new technologies, our entrepreneurs lacked this kind of mentorship.

At the time, Israeli companies could only secure venture funding from two sources. The first was a government grant-matching program run through the Office of the Chief Scientist, which, while well intended, was never able to provide new companies with sufficient funding to grow. The second was a similar program, the Binational Industrial Research and Development Foundation, known as BIRD Foundation, that had been created in 1977 as a joint fund between the United States and Israel. These grants, too, were modest, but they did something critical for us: they made it possible for Israeli companies to work closely with American partners—a joint venture in which the Israelis would invest in breakthrough innovations, while the Americans would invest in marketing and sales. Still, without a bustling private venture capital industry in Israel, it was clear that too few of our burgeoning companies would succeed, which meant too little economic benefit would accrue. Creating a venture capital industry would require two things: an internal effort to create local incentives, and an external effort to get investments flowing into the country.

The internal effort centered on a simple principle: the way to bring venture capital to Israel is to make Israel an unusually attractive place to invest. We had to change the equation. And so we designed two programs—one called Yozma (which means "initiative"), the other called Inbal (which means "tongue of the bell"). They were distinct in design but similar in their general ambition: the government would take ownership of most of the risk of an investment but cede all of the reward to investors. These programs ignited entrepreneurship in Israel in the early 1990s, creating the first wave of substantial venture capital.

Of course, creating this mechanism was only part of the solution. The other was finding the actual investors. This was the equivalent of a massive diplomatic effort, one I eagerly championed for decades. I saw it as my role—and obligation—to attract foreign investment to Israel. When I traveled to the United States, I pressed upon diaspora Jews that it was time to invest in Israeli start-ups, that it was up to them, as much as all of us, to transform the economy for good. As foreign minister, I established diplomatic relationships around the world in pursuit of economic collaboration. When I met with leaders in Europe, I pushed to connect Israel's state venture program to the government-supported funding mechanisms already in place in Europe. I spoke with those who might be open to importing Israeli technology for their own markets. When I met with the many hundreds of leaders of major companies, I would regale them with stories of the miracle of Israel, working to change their perception of the nation from only a tiny sliver of land in the desert to a cutting-edge technology powerhouse. In time, the strategy worked. The world's most respected venture funds started opening offices in Israel. Israelis began building dozens of venture funds of their own. I no longer had to convince anyone of the greatness of Israel's technology sector (not that it stopped me from telling the story). Israel's economic reputation finally matched its scientific might.

• • •

A nd yet, despite our success, standing still was not an option. There was a new argument to make now: not whether Israel was a high-tech leader, but where it should lead the world next.

Innovation, I understood, was not a mission to be completed, but a never-ending pursuit. We had created a system where investors were coming to us expecting pioneering technology. To keep them coming, we had to stay on the furthest frontier of science. As I've often said, it's not enough to be up to date. We have to be up "to-morrow."

And so, as I had done when I first discovered the computer and began to think about its military utility, I again turned to the research labs of Israel, taking countless meetings with scientists, reading journals and working papers, studying the latest developments, in search of the big idea that could set Israel apart.

It was through that process that I first learned about an emerging area of research that involved manipulating materials at the molecular level in an effort to assemble technology with atomic precision. It was called nanotechnology, and it was beyond anything I could have imagined. To begin with, scientists were working with matter the size of a nanometer, one hundred thousand of which could sit comfortable atop a single strand of human hair. Even more extraordinary, by working at the molecular level, scientists could develop materials that actually assembled themselves, in the very same way that molecules do all around us in nature—as when seeds turn into flowers in accordance with a biological code and scheme.

Nanotechnology was not destructive, but constructive—realigning atoms to produce new materials and new ways to store and generate energy. It reminded me of Israel—in something so tiny, that power of the miraculous.

And though the science was still emerging, the implications were vast. Nanotechnology could allow us to master every sort of matter, and shape its attributes as we desired: we could create something thinner than air, stronger than iron, lighter than feathers. It held the potential to make computers the size of the head of a pin; to make robots so small they could travel inside the body and attack cancerous cells; to make body armor many times stronger than steel, but weighing no more than a plastic bag. It was the equivalent of the lightbulb or the transistor: a new technology that would be a basis for its own industry—and transform every other. I believed I was witnessing the beginnings of the most important revolution of science and technology in my lifetime.

This was the future. Ben-Gurion once told me that government is responsible for everything that exists, and I was responsible for everything that doesn't. After more reading and research and conversations with experts, I decided that Israel must become the world leader in the development of nanotechnology. It was here, in this most minuscule of technologies, that I could see the grandest dreams of Israel becoming the centerpiece of the next scientific revolution, indispensable to all of the world.

I gathered my team right away to determine what would need to be done. What did we already have in place? What were we missing? What would it take to jump-start the effort?

What we learned was worrying. The following year, governments around the world were expected to invest more than $6 billion in nanotechnology research, with private companies expected to spend a similar amount. We had little time to spare. In the spring of 2002, I stood in the Knesset and gave the most impassioned speech I could deliver on the magic of nanotech, its scientific potential, the prosperity it could produce, and the risk in waiting to pursue it.

"In order to attract a greater number of qualified scientists, we will need qualified teams, outstanding students, better infrastructure and laboratories, better coordination of initiatives . . . new sources of funding, and better cooperation between industry and academia." And just as important, I added, we would need to "promote the opportunities presented by this initiative in the public consciousness." This was Israel's moon shot—not into outer space, but into inner space, the space between and among atoms. I pledged all of my energies to accomplish the mission.

Later that year, we created the Israel National Nanotechnology Initiative, known as INNI, and charged it with creating an engine for global leadership in the field. The INNI was instructed to engage with nanotechnology stakeholders around the world, from scientists to business leaders to venture capitalists; to establish funding priorities in Israel, with an eye toward bringing the science to a commercial phase faster; to help develop and procure the state-of-the-art infrastructure—manufacturing facilities, research centers, and equipment—that we would need to succeed; to encourage universities to collaborate with business, through the sharing of research and ideas; and finally, to fund-raise. Our estimates suggested that Israel would need a $300 million investment over five years to achieve our mission, and we expected the INNI to contribute a significant portion of that sum.

Over the years, I became something of a nanotechnology evangelist—the octogenarian enchanted by tech. I urged our researchers to embark on new efforts, speaking with passion to investors and donors and entrepreneurs about the possibilities I could see. During the Second Lebanon War in 2006, after seeing terrorists firing at civilian targets in Israel *from* civilian institutions in Lebanon (including mosques and hospitals), I was inspired to start a project that became known as Pearls of Wisdom. Its mission: to apply the breakthroughs of nano to our national defense in a new age of warfare. When I became president in 2007, I continued to raise awareness about the importance of the industry, urging greater collaboration and partnership between business and academia, working to get more ideas out of the lab and into the field. It didn't take long before I found inspiration again, in conversations with Israeli researchers about the potential of brain science. As with nanotechnology, I was moved by the idea that a single field of study could revolutionize so many different domains: that we could fundamentally change medicine, education, and computing by deciphering the mysteries of the brain. And so, in 2012, I helped to launch a new initiative—Israel Brain Technologies—which offered a million-dollar prize to an individual (or team) that could demonstrate an extraordinary breakthrough in the field.

When I left public office, I continued my work in technology, announcing the creation of the Israeli Innovation Center alongside my successor, President Reuven Rivlin, and Prime Minister Benjamin Netanyahu. Its ambition is to spark the imagination of every child; to empower the next generation to build a better world; and to demonstrate how far a people can come, in so short a period of time.

Indeed, among the six thousand start-ups based in Israel, there were ninety companies trading on the Nasdaq in 2016, valued at more than $40 billion. In 2014, Israel was second only to China among foreign firms listed on the exchange, and Tel Aviv ranked as having the second-best start-up ecosystem in the world, beaten out only by Silicon Valley. That same year, Israel jumped from thirtieth to fifth on the Bloomberg Innovation Index, beating out, among others, the United States and United Kingdom. Israeli high-tech companies continue to raise billions of dollars every year in investment.

Of course, the tech sector has driven more than just high growth; it has propelled a scientific revolution, with breakthroughs that have reverberated around the world. Who would have imagined that the world would run on USB drives invented in Israel, or that doctors could see inside patients with an Israeli-developed camera no larger than a pill? Who would have thought that the world would depend on Israeli technology for GPS navigation or that Israeli hardware and software could save drivers from deadly collisions? Who would have believed that medicines to treat Parkinson's disease and multiple sclerosis would have been developed right here, or that paralyzed people might be granted the ability to walk again through robotic legs invented in Israel? Ben-Gurion once said that in Israel, "in order to be a realist, you must believe in miracles." After such extraordinary achievement in science and technology and human creativity, how could we be anything but believers in miracles, faithful to the imaginations that are capable of conceiving them, and committed to the efforts to bring them to life? Ben-Gurion was right: realism in Israel is nothing less than the impossible made real.

CHAPTER 6

THE PURSUIT OF PEACE

In the early twentieth century, as World War I was raging, U.S. president Woodrow Wilson put forth a peace settlement proposal for the world, which became known as Wilson's Fourteen Points. Upon hearing of the list, the disbelieving French prime minister, Georges Clemenceau, reportedly responded, "Even God Almighty only has ten." I have spent most of the better part of my life in pursuit of peace, and in doing so have learned what Clemenceau didn't fully appreciate in that moment. Making peace is not a simple endeavor. It is a constant struggle. But its complexity should not overshadow its purpose.

Israel is a tiny island that, for most of its short existence, was surrounded by a sea of enemies. The wars we fought were forced upon us. In light of what our enemies hoped (and still hope) for, on the whole we have been triumphant, but we have yet to win the victory to which we have aspired: release from the need to win victories. Indeed, while we have proved that aggressors do not necessarily emerge as victors, we have also learned that victors do not necessarily win peace—that our work is not yet complete.

As a child I asked my grandfather which verse one should carry in one's heart. He recited to me the thirty-fourth chapter of the book of Psalms: "Whoever of you love life and desire to see many good days, keep your tongue from evil and your lips from telling lies. Seek peace and pursue it." And so I have, and so we must. I dedicated my life, first and foremost, to making sure Israel was secure: to protect her from the threat of destruction by working to build the greatest defense force in the world, and to deter our foes from believing she could ever be destroyed. When Israel was weak, I worked to make her fierce. But once she was strong, I gave my life's efforts to peace. Peace is, after all, our heart's truest desire, yet its pursuit must be based not just on political and economic concerns, but on moral and historical imperatives. As Ben-Gurion so often said, the moral high ground is also the basis of power.

The Jewish people have lived by the guiding principle of *tikkun olam*, the ambition to improve the whole world, not just ourselves. We lived in exile for two thousand years, without land, without independence, held together not by borders, but by this simple set of values that have echoed through history—in Hebrew, in Yiddish, in Ladino—in every language of every country into which the Jewish people dispersed. It is the basis of our identity. And it is from this moral code that we know, fundamentally, that Israel was not born to rule over other people, that to do so is in profound opposition to our heritage. And so I have pursued peace with all of my heart and soul, both realistically and optimistically, knowing its achievement remains our most essential task. Israel is small in territory, but it must be great in justice.

When I became prime minister in 1984, peace was my highest priority. Within my first four months in office, I executed a plan to withdraw our troops from Lebanon, where Israel had been fighting a misguided and fruitless war. But the economic emergency Israel faced took up the lion's share of my effort. By the time we had rescued our state from financial and fiscal calamity, our unity government had met its rotation deadline. Though many in my party insisted I not uphold my end of the bargain with Yitzhak Shamir, I have always been a man of my word. And so when the time came, I did what I had promised to do, stepping down into the role of foreign minister and ceding the prime minister's office to Shamir. I was no less committed to peace in my new role, nor any less willing to pursue it. But, as I would come to learn, doing so without the support of the prime minister would be the undoing of my first major attempt.

· · ·

The year was 1987. It had been nine years since Israeli prime minister Menachem Begin and Egyptian president Anwar Sadat signed the Camp David Accords, an achievement that few had believed possible. After three wars with the Egyptians, after nearly four decades in a constant state of conflict, after so much blood had been spilled and so much animosity calcified, the quest for peace was considered unimaginably naïve. And yet it was only four years after the end of the Yom Kippur War that Sadat made his visit to Israel, the breakthrough that would end in peace and partnership, a treaty signed and upheld to this day.

It was from that great victory for peace that I drew inspiration—to seek peace with the Jordanians and the Palestinians, thus ending another deadly conflict with our neighbors. I had envisioned something other than a two-state solution back then; it was what I called a tripartite solution, as it would include three autonomous areas: the State of Israel, the Kingdom of Jordan, and a joint entity in the West Bank for the Palestinian people, which would have its own parliament to run local affairs. In national affairs the Palestinians would have the right to vote, either in Israeli or Jordanian elections, depending on their citizenship.

My first overtures would be complicated. We had no diplomatic relations with Jordan. It was against the law to cross the border, to engage with the Jordanians personally or diplomatically in any way. Nearly our entire eastern border touched theirs, which made Israel vulnerable. Jordanian belligerence was a constant concern, a threat that argued for the necessity of peace. I believed it was time to begin the effort, however treacherous it might be.

And so I jumped in as best I could, trying to build a strategy that would start the conversation. The first move, I decided, was to place a phone call to a prominent London attorney named Victor Mishcon. Mishcon was a friend of mine and of Israel. He was also a friend of Jordan's King Hussein.

"Will you try to set up a meeting between King Hussein and me in London?" I asked unabashedly. There was a long pause on the other end of the line. "I will be happy to try, Shimon," he said, "but I don't want to get your hopes up. It would surprise me if he agreed to."

"Peace is always a long shot," I replied. "But that doesn't mean we shouldn't take the shot."

Several days later, I received a phone call from Mishcon, so eager he could barely contain himself. "Shimon, King Hussein has agreed!" he exclaimed. "I suggested the two of you have lunch at my house in London. He's eager to have the conversation!"

"I'm delighted to hear it, and for your discretion in hosting," I replied. "We are about to walk into a rare reality, and, perhaps, an even rarer opportunity."

By 1987, I had abdicated the position of prime minister to Yitzhak Shamir, as part of the unity government agreement we had struck. Though I was foreign minister and had broad authority, on something as sensitive as a secret meeting with Jordan, protocol demanded that I get Shamir's approval first. When I raised the plan with him, he didn't object—though not because he was interested in pursuing peace. Rather, he believed that any such attempt was hopeless, and that there was no harm in proving this to be true.

Accompanied by Yossi Beilin, the director of the ministry of foreign affairs, and a senior representative from Shamir's office, I landed in London in April 1987. We arrived at Mishcon's beautiful home, where we were greeted by King Hussein and Zaid Rifai, Jordan's prime minister. It was a surreal moment, shaking hands with sworn enemies in such an unassuming environment. But there was a power in it, too—the power to remind us that something extraordinary might be possible. For the sake of secrecy, Victor's wife had dismissed the staff and took on the task of hosting us, cooking a marvelous meal from scratch and serving it herself.

From the very beginning, Rifai seemed reluctant to be participating in any discussions of peace—even reluctant to break bread with the Jews across the table. It was clear he was not there on his own accord, but out of obligation to the king he served. Hussein, on the other hand, was warm and open from the moment we arrived. There was an excitement in his voice and his body language; I excitedly recognized a man who was gazing to the future with optimism and hope.

We sat around the table, in front of the beautiful lunch Mrs. Mishcon had prepared, and the king and I spoke to each other in English, not as enemies, but as newfound friends. We saw in each other a similar desire for a different relationship, and agreed that the moment was ripe to bring the conflict that had haunted our countries to an end. I had not arrived in London expecting such a reception—this was intended to be an initial overture, a chance to see if peace might eventually be possible. But as the conversation continued, it became increasingly clear that we had a chance, that very same day, to take a much more concrete step than I had imagined. As dusk settled onto misty London, Hussein and I had moved from broad strokes to concrete details, all with Rifai sitting in quiet frustration. When the meal was over, Mrs. Mishcon came in to clear the dishes.

"Let Mr. Peres and I do the dishes," Hussein said. "You've already done more than enough."

"Yes, that's a wonderful idea," I added. "Whenever Sonia cooks, I'm in charge of the dishes."

In the moment before Mrs. Mishcon could respond, I could already picture the scene, two former enemies, standing side by side as friends, the foreign minister of Israel in charge of scrubbing, the king of Jordan in charge of drying. It was an invitation to do something so simple, yet so intimate and meaningful and humble. But before we had the chance, Mrs. Mishcon interrupted.

"Absolutely not, gentlemen," she said firmly. "I would be mortified, and you have work to do."

We relented out of respect, and instead returned to our conversation. I suggested we put together a nonbinding conference for negotiations, one delegation from Israel, one representing both the Jordanians and the Palestinians. Hussein agreed.

"This is a holy challenge for me, a religious duty," he said. In that moment, I suddenly saw a direct line from the informal conversation we had undertaken to the signing of a peace treaty—and I believed I knew exactly how to get there. It was time to escalate our talks.

"In that case," I replied, "why don't we try to write down an agreement together, based on these discussions, right now?"

"I have another engagement I must go to," he replied, "but I can be back in an hour." In the meantime, he suggested that we should draft two documents: one describing the logistics of the peace conference, the other setting out the principles of agreement between our two countries. As soon as the king and prime minister left, we got to work. I dictated both documents as my aide typed feverishly. By the time Hussein and Rifai had returned, the first drafts of both documents were ready to be discussed.

When the Jordanians were finished reading the document, Rifai started listing the changes he wanted to make, but Hussein stopped him almost immediately. "These drafts reflect the agreement we discussed," he said. "I'm content to move forward." I was, admittedly, taken totally by surprise: the agreement we had put forward was quite fair to Israel. Not only did it create a path to peace with the Jordanians, it resolved the Palestinian question without requiring Israel to relinquish any of its territory or to change the status of Jerusalem.

The agreement stood in stark contrast to the order of the day, in which Jordan was a dangerous enemy interested in war, not peace. That we had made such progress at all was enchanting. That it had happened so quickly was inconceivable. In the course of a single day, it felt as if we had taken steps forward, that could be measured in years, to end a conflict that had lasted for decades.

Much like the Camp David Accords, we agreed it would be helpful to have the United States put forward the proposal as a distinctly American one, allowing each side to agree to it without revealing the secret negotiations from which it had been born. We would send it to George Shultz, the secretary of state, and ask him to present it back to us.

I flew home that night brimming with delight. In the thirty years since, we have never come close to achieving peace with so few concessions.

I phoned Shamir as soon as I landed, and we agreed to meet alone, after the weekly cabinet session. As we sat together, I described the improbable experience of the previous day, giving him a detailed account of the conversation with the king and prime minister, and the documents we had produced. I read each to him, expecting him to light up in similar joy. But he sat quietly, seemingly unmoved. He asked me to read them to him again, and again I did. Still, there was no emotion on his face. He had not expected such a breakthrough, and it was suddenly clear to me that he hadn't wanted one to begin with. He had approved the conversation believing it was doomed, and that I, the dreamer, the fantasizer, was the perfect fool for the job.

Engaging in peace talks is like being a pilot. The mother wants him to fly low and slow, out of fear for his safety. But this is precisely how a plane falls out of the sky. In order to make peace, one must fly high and fast; it is the only way to avoid a crash. I know, from decades of experience, the consequences of both. Now I feared that Shamir had always intended my ascent to be a slight one.

Shamir asked me to leave the documents with him, but I was concerned about doing so. If their contents leaked, it would scuttle the agreement. Besides, I told him, it would be better if the prime minister received the draft documents from the Americans, to reinforce the notion that it was their proposal we were considering, not our own. Neither this, nor any part of our conversation, appeared to sit well with the prime minister, and I left the meeting with a knot in my stomach. Could it really be possible, I wondered, that a moment such as this could be squandered? Was the man who became prime minister only a few months earlier ready to sully the deal?

The tragic answer was that he was. Without consulting me, he sent Minister Moshe Arens to Washington to meet with Shultz. Arens explained that if the United States were to present the draft agreement, Shamir would view it as an inappropriate interference in Israel's geopolitical affairs. Upon hearing this, Shultz concluded that there was no good reason to present the agreements. Why go out on a limb if Shamir was sure to break it?

I learned of the meeting, and its outcome, after the fact. It was a slap in the face to me personally, and a punch in the gut to the country I loved. Ben-Gurion had been gone for nearly fifteen years, but there was never a time I had missed him more. He would have embraced the breakthrough; Shamir strangled it before it could have the chance to breathe. I made one last attempt to save the deal, pleading with Shultz to reconsider. But even as Shultz grew open to it, it was clear that Hussein had closed the door. Where I felt deeply disappointed, the king felt indelibly betrayed. He had taken a sizable risk and, for it, received nothing in return. He had little interest in rekindling the conversation. The London Agreement, as it became known, was dead. What a devastating blow it was to the State of Israel, and to our efforts at seeking peace and cooperation with our neighbors.

The next five years were difficult for Israel and for the Palestinians. Shamir and his Likud party did nothing to further the peace process, save for a halfhearted participation in an international conference in Madrid. In the meantime, a violent uprising called the first intifada began in the West Bank and Gaza, leaving the streets stained with blood, and a country racked by fear and frustration. The masterpiece that the London Agreement could have been was replaced instead by the ugliness of violence, the disfiguration of war. And yet we persevered, as leaders must, knowing that no door stays shut forever—that with concerted effort, even the heaviest can be pried open.

In 1992, those efforts bore fruit. The Likud party was thrown out of power, and Labor once again took the reins of government. Yitzhak Rabin and I ran against each other in the interparty elections for prime minister. We knew the outcome would be close and so we met before the vote and made a deal: whoever was voted in as prime minister would appoint the other foreign minister. We had been political rivals, of course, but we also believed in each other's leadership capabilities, and the value that would come from our working close together. We were like two great boxers, allies at odds, with great respect for the other even when we often disagreed. He was deeply granular in his thinking, focused intensely on the details in front of him. My head was always tilted higher, toward the horizon and beyond it. We were different in so many ways, but in ways that made the other stronger, smarter, and wiser. In time, the rivalry became a partnership.

When the votes were tallied, Rabin had narrowly won. It was hard not to be disappointed, but it was the work more than the position that captured my focus. It is hard to escape one's ego, but I've seen in others that the greatest accomplishments come from recognizing that the task at hand matters far more than the title. After the election was over, I went to Rabin to congratulate him and to offer myself as a true partner in the efforts to come. "If you will go and work for peace, you won't have a more loyal friend than me," I told him. "But," I warned, "if you turn your back on peace, you will have no worse enemy than me." I explained that I believed we had arrived at a unique moment. The fall of the Soviet Union in 1991 had fundamentally altered the world order, changing the circumstances in the Middle East in a powerful way. For nearly all of our state's existence, our Arab neighbors had seemingly unlimited access to military and political support from the Soviet Union. With its collapse, suddenly they had neither, creating a paradigm shift in the region.

At the same time, the unity of the Arab world began to crumble, as Iraq invaded Kuwait, and an international coalition that included Arab nations took up arms against Saddam Hussein's regime. The possibility of progress took on a new and hopeful character. But with the "Jordanian option" no longer on the table, we were faced with a difficult question: With whom should Israel negotiate?

The Palestine Liberation Organization certainly was an option, but a deeply controversial one. Founded in 1964, the group was an organized collective of terrorist organizations that had declared and perpetuated a campaign of horrific violence against Israeli civilians and soldiers in hope of bringing about Israel's ultimate destruction. For more than three decades the PLO had launched attacks from bases in the West Bank, Gaza, Lebanon, Jordan, and Syria, indiscriminately targeting the innocent far away from any battlefield. They attacked a school bus in 1970, murdering nine children, then four years later seized a school and massacred twenty-seven students and adults. They were behind the hijacking of airplanes and hostage standoffs in hotels, along with the brutal killings of eleven Israeli Olympians in Munich in 1972. When the first intifada began in 1987, the PLO played a lead role in organizing and encouraging the bloodshed. And yet, despite the seemingly endless violence, the PLO remained the primary representative of the Palestinian people, having earned broad popular support. Its chairman, Yasser Arafat, was likely the most influential person with whom we could negotiate peace, but he was, first and foremost, a terrorist, a murderer of children, and the idea of sitting across the table from him was, for all of us, a hard thing to imagine.

And yet, over time, it became clear that negotiating with Arafat would be the only prospect for peace. When Rabin and I assumed office, Israel was engaged in fruitless discussions in Washington with a Jordanian-Palestinian delegation. Technically, the Palestinian team did not include any members of the PLO. And yet in truth, a number of the negotiators in Washington were formerly members of that terrorist organization and, most important, were taking their orders directly from Arafat, then based in Tunisia. During negotiating sessions, this made the Palestinian negotiators impossibly cautious, unwilling to cede any ground or accept any terms without Arafat's explicit approval. Thus, despite the best efforts of the Americans, the process started already mired in inertia—and remained that way throughout.

"Look, everything we talk to the Palestinians about, they send a fax to Arafat," I said to my staff, while airing my frustrations about the lack of progress. "I'm fed up with negotiating by fax machine."

"What do you propose we do?" asked one of my advisors.

"I'm going to talk to Rabin," I said. "I think it's time to start negotiations with the PLO directly."

I didn't come to the decision easily. Neither Rabin nor I was eager to start peace negotiations with a terrorist organization. Doing so would force us to confront fundamental moral dilemmas, and daunting political challenges at home. Direct contact with the PLO was technically unlawful, but even if it weren't, it was likely to be universally unpopular. Arafat was a household name in Israel, easily the most hated person in our country. To directly engage such a man risked the appearance of betrayal. And yet at the same time, I knew that Rabin and I were not there to do nothing in exchange for popularity. The security of Israel and the future of its people depended on our willingness to seek peace. And no peace process can begin until enemies are first willing to engage with one another.

And so I went to Rabin's office to make the case for a change in our strategy. I argued that out of necessity we should begin negotiations with the PLO in secret, but that we would not come to an agreement of any kind until Arafat publicly and forcefully denounced terrorism and demanded an end to violence. If we were going to shake hands with a terrorist organization, we would only do so once they gave up terror for good.

Rabin was skeptical at first, believing that the negotiations in Washington would eventually turn productive. But soon his frustrations about the stalemate of those talks led him to the same conclusion at which I had arrived: if we were going to have a chance at peace, we'd have to be willing to travel an alternate path. We knew how fraught such a choice would be, that even the act of sitting across from the PLO would risk legitimizing an organization that, as its core tenet, sought the destruction of our state. And yet we also knew an unavoidable truth: One does not make peace with one's friends. If peace is what we seek, we must have the courage to pursue it with our enemy.

. . .

In the early 1990s, three academics—Terje Rød-Larsen of Norway and Yair Hirschfeld and Ron Pundak of Israel—started having direct conversations with members of the PLO about the prospect of making peace with Israel. This was a "track two" negotiation, one done informally and largely for the purpose of identifying possibilities for action. Yossi Beilin, by then my deputy, had been made aware of these conversations through back channels with Rød-Larsen and had been kept apprised of developments as they unfolded. For a time, not much had come from them. But by the spring of 1993, we had learned that a close confidant of Arafat, a man named Abu Ala'a, had joined the discussion about whether and how a peace agreement might be reached.

In the preceding years, the PLO had been thrown out of Jordan, and later driven out of Lebanon, which had forced it to relocate its headquarters to Tunisia. After a decade in which the group's exile moved it farther and farther from Gaza and the West Bank, the PLO leadership had lost its connection to the Palestinians living in those places. As the organization began to wither, its leadership started to consider something unthinkable among its ranks: that peace with Israel might be its only way to regain power and influence. Indeed, Abu Ala'a expressed far greater willingness than we could have predicted to make the critical concessions that a peace process would require. We were told that he and his fellow negotiators had already floated a number of imaginative ideas with the Norwegians, confirming my impression, contra the Washington talks, that the PLO was in fact looking to strike a deal.

"We should enter the conversation," I said. "I'll need to talk to Rabin."

I believed that negotiations would need to occur in stages if they were to be successful. To enter such discussions with the expectation that all issues would be resolved at once was to expect both the impossible and the unnecessary. Our goal was peace, but that did not mean peace at an infeasible pace. I argued that the goal of the negotiation should be to define a set of mutually agreed-upon principles, a set of promises each side would make to the other. On issues where we found agreement, we would set timetables for their implementations. On those unresolved, we would set timetables for future negotiations.

Rabin and I discussed our ambitions for such a declaration. Without question, we would demand that the PLO renounce terror and recognize our right to exist—and to exist in peace. We would demand that, under any circumstance that involved returning land, Israel would retain both its exclusive ability to control its own borders, and the unquestioned authority to defend itself against threats. In exchange for these commitments, we would propose a gradual process: withdrawing from Gaza and the Jericho area of the West Bank first.

Of critical importance, we believed, was bringing Arafat from Tunis to Gaza, and establishing a Palestinian Council, which he would seek to run pending an internationally supervised election. Though the peace process could start with the PLO, permanent status would only be achievable if we had a negotiating partner that represented the Palestinian people, rather than the factions among them who demanded more and more violence.

After multiple conversations, Rabin agreed that it was worth moving forward. I invited Avi Gil, my chief of staff, and Uri Savir, the Foreign Ministry's director general, to my official residence in Jerusalem. Avi and I were discussing the situation when Uri arrived.

"What can I do for you?" Uri asked.

"How do you feel about a weekend in Oslo?" I replied.

"Excuse me?" he said with a stunned expression, not because he didn't understand the request, but because he surely did.

I spent the rest of the afternoon defining the strategy for the initial session, peppering Avi with questions about every detail of our approach, which he and I had been coordinating for weeks. We laid out our goals, both ultimate and immediate, and briefed Uri with strict instructions about how we expected him to conduct the initial conversations.

"When you return, based on your report, we'll decide how you should proceed," I told him.

Uri left for Oslo shortly after and returned with a hopeful assessment. Abu Ala'a, the chief negotiator of the PLO, had seemed eager to find agreement. "I believe we've arrived at the root of the problem," Abu Ala'a told Uri. "We have learned that our rejection of you will not bring us freedom. And you have learned that control of us will not bring you security. We must live side by side in peace, equality, and cooperation." In the report he delivered later to Rabin and me, Uri wrote that while we know everything about the Palestinians, it seemed we understood nothing. It was in that space—in the seeking of deeper understanding, in the mutual reaching for empathy across the divide—that I believed peace might very well take root.

Over the course of the summer, the negotiating teams returned to the lodge to push the effort forward, reporting progress back to me, while they awaited my further instruction. As in any negotiation, there were bumps and breakthroughs, important steps forward followed by frustrating setbacks. There were times when it seemed that even these negotiators, who had formed a special bond, would be unable to overcome impasses. Though the discussions had moved much further along than their Washington counterpart, an inability to come to terms would represent just as painful a failure.

But by early August 1993, negotiations had proceeded so well that we believed a declaration of principles could be reached in the next meeting, which would start on the thirteenth of August. Two days into the session, Arafat told us that he was ready to sign the declaration, assuming we could work out final language on a few outstanding issues. Both negotiating teams believed we would be able to find a meeting of the minds; the breakthrough we had dreamed of seemed to be just within our grasp. After hearing the news, I spent the entire night wide awake, unable to slow the gears spinning around and around in my brain. Though I had spent so much of my life with my eyes fixed on the future, in those sleepless hours it was the past that had overtaken my mind. I thought back to the first time I'd met Ben-Gurion, the first time he'd given me a chance to be part of something so much bigger than myself. I thought back to the wars, the loss, the fear, and the uncertainty, to the days of hunger and insecurity, to the questions of our very survival. I thought of Dimona, and the path its deterrent power had created. I thought of the extraordinary work of the IDF, how critical our military strength had been to make this moment possible. And I heard again, in my head, the words of Ben-Gurion: "In Israel, in order to be a realist, you must believe in miracles."

That morning, I walked into work with eyes that revealed deep exhaustion, but a mind that was racing, energized by the thrill of the work at hand. I opened the door to my office and turned on the lights only to be startled by the shouts of "Surprise!" A small group of staff and close friends were waiting for me. It was only then that I realized it was my seventieth birthday.

It was a beautiful moment of kindness and warmth, even more so given the circumstances. These were people who had worked so hard by my side and in doing so had claimed ownership over a big piece of my heart. They shared my passion for dreaming, the desire to take on the improbable, and they chased the future with a fervor and focus that left me eternally grateful. The negotiations were still a secret, even to them, but I hoped to share good news with them as soon as I could. In the meantime, I thanked them for all they had done. "I have devoted most of my life to security," I told them. "What's left to me, now that Israel is strong, is to bring our young people to peace."

I left the party and went straight into a meeting with Rabin to discuss our next steps. The staff-level negotiations would take us only so far; I believed it was time for me to enter the negotiations directly, in my official capacity as foreign minister.

I told Rabin that I already had a prescheduled trip to Scandinavia, where I'd been invited to make official visits to Sweden and Norway. I suggested that I use the timing as an opportunity to join the talks myself so that I could close the negotiations on the outstanding issues. My goal, I said, was to get both teams to initial an agreement before I returned home. When negotiations had first begun, Rabin had wanted me to avoid direct contact, believing that doing so could commit the cabinet—and the country—to a negotiation that was still unknown to all of them. But now, as we stood precariously, yet with an agreement so close in our sights, Rabin had become convinced it was time to step up our efforts.

I arrived in Stockholm with Avi, and was soon joined by Rød-Larsen and Johan Jørgen Holst, the Norwegian foreign minister. The idea was to get Abu Ala'a on the phone, to let him know I was there, ready to negotiate, and that he and Holst would need to serve as the liaisons between Arafat and me. Rød-Larsen finally got in touch with Abu Ala'a shortly after 1:00 A.M.

Holst took the phone from Rød-Larsen and, with me sitting next to him, read through the proposed changes in language, most of which involved slight tweaks of wording, and greater clarity in certain passages. When he was finished, he hung up the phone and told us that Abu Ala'a had asked for ninety minutes to discuss the changes with Arafat. The conversation resumed and continued over a series of short phone calls through the early hours of the morning. By 4:30 A.M., we had done what so many had assumed would never happen: come to terms on a Declaration of Principles between Israel and the PLO. We could hear cheers over the phone line as the negotiators in Arafat's office burst into shouts and applause. The same emotions that had overcome them had taken the rest of us, too. It was a moment I'll never forget.

I woke up feeling jubilant the next morning, but those feelings were quickly set aside as I received distressing news. A roadside bomb in Lebanon had killed seven Israeli soldiers. I phoned Rabin to discuss the tragedy. "We are on the verge of something historic," I told him. "But I fear this news may change the atmosphere for the worse on both sides. Perhaps we should postpone." Rabin was similarly concerned, but he felt that delay was not an option—there was simply not enough time. We proceeded as planned.

The next day, my trip brought me to Norway, where I was put up in a Norwegian government guesthouse. I went through the motions of my official schedule, including a dinner in my honor. As the meal wound down, I excused myself, noting that I was still quite jet-lagged from the journey, but as soon as I got back to the guesthouse I slipped away from my entourage to witness the secret signing ceremony of the Declaration of Principles. All the relevant players had relocated to Norway, given Holst's central role in forging the agreement; here, so far from the Middle Eastern sun and sand, and so far from expectations, enemies would clasp hands. It was a beautiful—and emotional—moment.

I was not to sign myself; the Israeli government had yet to approve the documents. Instead, negotiators from both sides were to initial the declaration, and in doing so, set us on a course toward a formal agreement. And so it went: the extraordinary and improbable work of both teams was now represented in a declaration that had the power to change the course of our history. To see all of these men together, tears in their eyes and smiles on their faces, was a reminder that, for all of our differences and despite a harrowing past, we believed a better, safer, more peaceful future was not only possible, but essential. I struggled to restrain my own emotions as I watched the moment unfold, fighting back joyful tears for the sake of appearing diplomatic.

When the signing was over, each member of the negotiating teams spoke. Abu Ala'a said something I'll never forget: "The future that we look for will not materialize unless we together overcome the fears of the past and learn from the past lessons for our future." When the remarks portion was finished, Abu Ala'a came over to me to introduce himself. It was the first time I'd had a conversation with a member of the PLO directly. "I have keenly followed your declarations, statements, and writings," he said, "which confirmed to us your desire to achieve a just, permanent, and comprehensive peace." We retired to a separate room, just the two of us, and spent thirty minutes speaking alone in English, our common language. I impressed upon him our commitment to the agreement, and I told him he would have my help, and the help of the international community, in providing economic assistance to the blossoming Palestinian project.

And yet I knew that this effort was still far from official. There was critical work that still had to be done. First, I would need to go to the United States to personally inform Secretary of State Warren Christopher of our breakthrough, to make sure we would have the support of the Americans. There were some among us who feared that they would be angry at not having been included in the negotiation—though they knew it was under way—or that the work of our track had undercut their own efforts. Without America's support, I doubted we could hold the process together, or undertake the future negotiations the Declaration of Principles demanded.

I left Israel for the United States on August 28. Christopher was vacationing in California, so we arranged to meet him at the Point Mugu Naval Air Station, just off the Pacific Coast. Dennis Ross, the head of the United States' peace team, flew to join us there, as well. I greeted them both with excitement in my heart, and tried to convey my hopefulness in words. When I told them we had signed off on a Declaration of Principles, they were stunned, both eager to see the document. I stood there patiently as they read it, and watched their disbelief disappear before my eyes.

"Dennis, what do you think?" asked Christopher, before giving me his own comments.

"I think this is a great historic achievement," Ross responded with enthusiasm.

"Absolutely!" replied Christopher, a grand smile on his face.

I wanted the United States to adopt the Declaration of Principles as its own initiative, and requested that we hold the signing ceremony at the White House. I also had another document to share.

"There's more," I told them. "We've been working in parallel on the issue of mutual recognition, and I believe we will soon have a deal."

From the beginning of negotiations, I believed that mutual recognition was essential, that we needed to reach a point where each side could affirm the legitimacy of the other. I was well aware of the challenges that required us to overcome. The PLO would need not only to transform itself, but to reverse itself, to walk away from its founding principles and disavow the terrorism that had been its primary weapon. We, too, would have to accord the PLO and the Palestinians a respect we had not previously extended. The demands of mutual recognition struck at the very ideology that had been at the center of our conflict, and were different, in kind, than those of the Declaration of Principles. Whereas the declaration set goals and defined timetables for future negotiation, the demands of mutual recognition were—with the exception of wording—fundamentally nonnegotiable.

By the time I showed our list of points to Christopher and Ross, we were close to an agreement on mutual recognition. Again, the Americans were stunned by how far we had come.

"You've done a tremendous job," Christopher said. "My initial response to these developments is very, very positive." He and Ross agreed that we should move forward with a week of intensive negotiations. And they suggested that if Israel reached a point where it could recognize the PLO, the United States would likely do the same.

For several days in September, we held firm on our list of demands. In exchange for Israel recognizing the PLO as a legitimate representative of the Palestinian people, Arafat would need to recognize Israel's right to exist, unconditionally; deliver a full-throated renunciation of terrorism; call for an immediate halt to the intifada; and provide a firm commitment to resolve future conflicts through peaceful negotiation rather than violence.

By the afternoon of September 7, 1993, Arafat was ready to accept our demands. Two letters were drafted, one for Arafat, recognizing Israel's right to exist, the other for Rabin, recognizing the PLO as the legitimate representative of the Palestinian people.

Rabin and I received them by fax in Jerusalem, as Arafat received them in Tunis. Rabin received approval from the cabinet to sign the letter, while Arafat received the same approval from the PLO Executive Committee. In the early-morning hours of September 10, the Norwegian foreign minister brought the letters to the prime minister's office, which had been filled with journalists and cameras. Holst took his seat on one side of Rabin and I sat on the other as we, and the world, watched him affix his signature to the simply stated letter. The PLO had recognized our right to exist, and in return, Israel had done the same.

Three days later, on September 13, 1993, mutual recognition was celebrated in a poignant expression on the South Lawn of the White House, in a handshake that was watched—and remembered—the world over. Yitzhak Rabin and Yasser Arafat had never imagined they would find themselves in such a situation, but there they stood, under the bright summer sun, as President Clinton pulled them closer together. Rabin shook the hand of his sworn enemy with some reluctance. He saw the promise of peace, and the size of the momentous achievement, but he still recoiled at what was required. During the accompanying applause, he turned to me and whispered, "Now it's your turn."

Moments later, in front of a crowded South Lawn, and with cameras of every international news organization imaginable, I took a seat at a wooden table, picked up a pen, and signed my name to the Declaration of Principles—on behalf of the country I always believed in, and with the hope for a brighter future.

. . .

After several days of working sessions in Washington, D.C., I flew back to Israel with the negotiating team, arriving at the airport just after 4:00 A.M.

"Be in my office at seven," I told the group. "The work is only beginning."

They arrived for the meeting exhausted, only to find me eager to keep them going.

"It's time to storm Jordan!" I exclaimed. They laughed heartily, at first, assuming—or at least hoping—that I was telling a joke. But it took only a moment for them to realize I was serious, and to make the case that, this time, my dreams needed reining in. They argued that the opportunity for peace with the kingdom was terribly unlikely, that we had seen little movement or willingness to reengage the conversation. And given that the basis for both the failed London Agreement and the disappointing Washington talks had centered on a joint solution with Jordan and the Palestinians, the team felt that Jordan would be particularly frustrated to have been left out of the peace process.

I knew the arguments well, but I disagreed. Perhaps King Hussein would indeed be irked about the bilateral nature of our agreement with the Palestinians. But that agitation, I believed, was more likely to lead to engagement than isolation. For many years, the king had maintained relationships in Jerusalem that were important to his ultimate goals. But if our efforts succeeded—if we were to reach comprehensive peace with the Palestinians—Hussein would fear losing his influence, being replaced, in essence, by Arafat. The strategic considerations, in such a case, would likely outweigh his personal frustrations.

"Trust me," I told my team. "The king won't want to be left behind."

I also felt that if the king were willing to engage in direct talks, we were likely to come to a favorable agreement rather quickly. When Hussein and I worked out the details of the London Agreement, it was clear that I was sitting across the table from a man who saw the power and necessity of peace. His willingness to accept my terms, despite his doubts, was surely a reflection of this view.

My team went to work immediately, developing the framework for discussions in Jordan's capital, Amman—everything from the planning and logistics of an initial meeting to the contours of a peace agreement we would find acceptable. In the meantime, I approached Rabin to seek his opinion—and ultimately, his approval. Like my negotiating team, Rabin was skeptical. He had spoken to King Hussein on October 19, 1993, and was immediately rebuffed when he raised the prospect of a peace treaty. Hussein suggested he consider a series of interim agreements, but comprehensive peace was out of the question. Even so, I told Rabin I believed I could make a deal, and asked for his blessing to try. Skeptical though he was, Rabin agreed.

I spoke with the Americans as well, and was once again told that I was flying a bit too close to the sun. Even if I could make progress with Hussein, they thought Syria would be an obstacle. President Hafez al-Assad had made clear to his fellow Arab states that any discussion of peace needed to be done as a region, that separate deals between individual countries and Israel were simply unacceptable. Given the geopolitical situation, the Americans believed Assad could stop our progress in its tracks. And yet they too offered their help—including the possibility of serving as mediators—if it turned out my fantasy was closer to reality than they imagined.

On the first day of November 1993, I donned a hat and fake mustache. Because we lacked relations with Jordan—and were technically still in a state of war—Avi Gil and I, along with Efraim Halevy, the deputy director of Mossad, would have to make our way to the royal palace in secret. I couldn't help but laugh as I glued the mustache to my face. Nor could I help but feel the pull of the past. I thought back to the sunglasses we put on Moshe Dayan in place of his distinctive eye patch; of the wide-brimmed hat we affixed to Ben-Gurion's head to hide his characteristically chaotic white hair. How many times in my life had we put on such silly disguises in pursuit of something that others were certain was impossible? These were some of the very best memories of my relative youth. And knowing at seventy that I was still in the fight, still battling for the future of Israel, gave the mustache a certain power. I looked like an actor in a low-budget stage show, but I felt like the tip of the spear.

We drove across the Allenby Bridge and into Jordanian territory, eventually arriving at the Royal Court, situated atop a hill in the old sector of Amman. We were escorted to Raghadan Palace (one of many in the king's court), which shared the same Islamic features of the architecture one could find in east Jerusalem. We were brought to Throne Hall, its vaulted ceilings decorated with intricate art from the Arab world, where we were greeted by the king. I made sure to remove my fake mustache before the conversation began.

It had been seven long years since Hussein and I sat together with such an important mission before us. Yet from the moment the conversation began, it felt like it had never quite ended. We treated each other as old friends, and found once again a common view of the future. Though there were central political issues that had to be discussed and overcome, I decided the best approach was to bypass them by focusing the king's attention on a new economic vision for the Middle East.

I spoke at great length about my dream, not just of peace in the region, but of prosperity, too, and promised the same kind of economic assistance that I had pledged the Palestinians. "Israel does not want to be an island of wealth in a sea of poverty," I told him. "And though we have no interest in meddling in your internal affairs, we are willing—and eager—to help." Among my suggestions was that Israel launch an initiative to invite thousands of corporate leaders from around the world to Amman to discuss investing in Jordan, one of many critical steps that could remake the Middle East over time. I described a vision of partnership and friendship across borders, one that would offer untold benefits to both of our countries. I asked him to imagine foreign investment pouring into the Middle East, creating the economic prosperity that was a prerequisite for lasting stability. Hussein was enthusiastic about the prospect, enough so that he agreed to let me step away so that we could put a framework on paper. Avi, Efraim, and I retired to a nearby room.

"Help me with this," I asked Efraim, who proceeded to work with me on a four-page document that defined the parameters of a future peace agreement. I asked Avi to review the terms and offer his counsel and input. When the document was completed, I sent Efraim back to the Jordanians to present what I had dictated.

To my delight, the Jordanians offered minor changes, but accepted the terms as I had laid them out. In addition to the establishment of the economic conference, the agreement, which we termed a "nonpaper," included the establishment of two international committees: one to deal with the issue of refugees, another to develop solutions to the political and territorial issues that would need to be overcome to reach a true peace treaty.

On November 2, King Hussein and I shook hands and affixed our signatures to the handwritten document, setting the stage for further and deeper discussions that would carve a path to a new and necessary future. Hussein's only request was that we keep the agreement secret. We readily agreed.

Avi, Efraim, and I left Amman filled with hopeful momentum, deeply encouraged both by the progress we'd made and the pace at which we'd achieved it. I felt as though I were living in a dream, one of my own creation, confident for the first time in years that the dashed London Agreement had not been our only chance for a lasting peace with our neighbor. I couldn't stop smiling as Avi and I regaled one another with the achievements of the day. I was more excited than at any time I could remember since childhood, filled with relief and hope and pride. My elation enveloped me, more perhaps than is wise. In a rare moment in a long career of absolute secrecy, it caused me to make a careless mistake.

I had arrived at a television studio to provide a routine interview as foreign minister. "Remember November the second!" I said with delight while waiting in the "green room," thinking back to the extraordinary day. I thought it was sufficiently cryptic, nothing more than a throwaway line. I turned out to be wrong.

Unbeknownst to me, I had been overheard by journalists, some of whom were somehow able to interpret my remarks. They concluded that an agreement must have been reached and that I must have been in Jordan. I didn't know I had committed an error until the peace talks were leaked to the media as an unconfirmed rumor. King Hussein was understandably furious that his request had not been honored, and was concerned about the consequences for Jordan at home. It was enough for him to call off the peace process—enough to strand our historic breakthrough.

With our agreement suddenly in peril, it seemed clear there was only one way to save it: Rabin would need to take the lead on the remaining negotiations, and I would have to retreat behind the scenes. I was disappointed: in myself for having slipped, and in the result. But my sights never wavered from the goal of peace.

By May 1994, a calmed and again optimistic Hussein was back at the negotiating table, with Rabin sitting across from him. Because Hussein and I had already negotiated the core terms of an agreement, the peace process, once restarted, moved with impressive speed. On July 25, Rabin and Hussein joined Clinton in Washington for the signing of a nonbelligerence pact, declaring the end of hostilities between our two countries and calling for a negotiation that would lead to a peace treaty. For the rest of the summer and into the fall, teams from Jordan and Israel held a number of negotiating sessions to finalize the agreement. By the end of October, a genuine peace was at hand: on a blistering hot day in the Arava Valley, not far from Eilat, on the rim of the Red Sea, at the crossing between Jordan and Israel, five thousand guests joined us for the signing of a treaty that would officially end forty-six years of war. President Clinton was there to witness the moment, and to offer a few words of inspiration.

"This vast, bleak desert hides great signs of life," he said. "Today we see the proof of it, for peace between Jordan and Israel is no longer a mirage. It is real. It will take root in this soil."

When it was Hussein's turn to speak, he described our achievement as "peace with dignity" and "peace with commitment."

"This is our gift to our peoples and the generations to come," he exclaimed to the audience.

Rabin used the moment to call not just for peace, but for unity. "We have known many days of sorrow, and you have known many days of grief," he said. "But bereavement unites us, as does bravery, and we honor those who sacrificed their lives. We both must draw on the springs of our great spiritual resources, to forgive the anguish we caused each other, to clear the minefields that divided us for so many years and to supplant them with fields of plenty."

I spoke only briefly: to thank President Clinton for his support; to thank King Hussein for his trust; and, most important, to thank Prime Minister Rabin for his leadership.

"I shall do something improper and tell you about my own prime minister. He did a great job, with great courage and wisdom," I remarked of Rabin. I added that it was in our dogged pursuit of peace that we had become more than colleagues; we had become kin. "We were born as sons of Abraham," I said. "Now we have become brothers in the family of Abraham."

Less than a week later, the promise I had made to King Hussein to bring together business leaders from around the world was realized—albeit hosted not in Jordan but in Morocco. During the year leading up to the peace treaty, none of my advisors believed that such an event would come to pass. Yet now the Middle East/North Africa Economic Summit opened in Casablanca with four thousand participants. It was the first time that Israelis and Arabs had the chance to meet together, not to negotiate peace politically, nor to keep peace militarily, but to build peace economically.

King Hassan II of Morocco had made available a special tent for King Hussein and me, where the leadership of more than a dozen Arab countries—along with leaders and businessmen from more than fifty other countries—could meet with us, and speak about their hopes, their aspirations, and their immediate needs in developing a New Middle East. What became instantly clear was that our efforts at peace had not just made collaboration with the Palestinians and Jordanians possible; it had opened up the entire region.

"The entire world is gradually evolving from a universe of enemies into an arena of opportunities and challenges," I said in remarks to the conference attendees. "If yesterday's enemy was an army threatening from without, today's source of violence is principally the menace from within: poverty breeding despair.

"This is not a new philanthropy," I emphasized. "This is a new business strategy, using purely economic logic. . . . Here in Casablanca, we are entrusted with the obligation to take the first step in transforming the Middle East—from a hunting ground into a field of creativity."

. . .

The march toward peace continued. We held several follow-up negotiations with the Palestinians, as prescribed in the Declaration of Principles. In May 1994, we signed the Gaza-Jericho agreement, which, among other things, established the Palestinian

Authority. Within two months, Arafat returned to Gaza, where he was elected the Palestinian Authority's first president. In September 1995, we signed an interim agreement with the Palestinians, known as Oslo II, which expanded Palestinian self-government in the West Bank, while setting May 1996 as the latest date at which negotiations over a permanent solution would begin.

But in spite of our progress, the mood had darkened throughout Israel. In its willingness to seek a peace agreement with the Israelis, the Palestinian Authority had made enemies of radical terrorist organizations that rejected any peace negotiation with Israel as illegitimate. Hamas and Islamic Jihad, whose leadership was furious at the prospect of any Israeli-Palestinian agreement, attempted to undermine the peace process through continual acts of unspeakable violence, including sending suicide bombers onto buses and into crowded neighborhoods and big cities, directly targeting civilians. The Palestinian leadership didn't put a stop to the attacks. In some cases, they even helped coordinate them. There were bombings in April 1994 and then again in October and November, and then again in January 1995 and April and August. A growing coalition of Israelis, having abandoned hope for peace, had starting calling instead for a military response. There were protests and demonstrations, chants of "Death to Arabs" and "Death to Arafat" echoing through the streets, and demands not only for small-scale retribution but for war itself.

These conditions created an enormous leadership challenge for Rabin and me. The hope that sprang from Oslo was increasingly hidden from view, receding among some, dying among others. Women and children were being murdered in the streets, and yet we were still involved in ongoing negotiations, still working with a faction of Palestinians who understood the imperative of peace. We couldn't abandon the effort, not after how far we had come, not after the commitment we had made to the children of Israel, and to those not yet born. And so we pressed on, together, with the understanding that if we were voted out of power, it would be because we stood up for Jewish values even in the face of impossible odds.

After so many years of rivalry and partnership, it was only during that summer that my respect for Rabin would become genuine admiration. He and I had become targets of vile attacks, not just in the media, but on the streets. Opponents dressed our effigies in Nazi uniforms and burned them. They marched in droves through the streets, at one point carrying a coffin meant for Rabin. It was horrifying.

I remember being told about one particularly shocking moment, as Rabin walked past the Wingate Institute in Netanya, between Haifa and Tel Aviv. The gathered crowd began to shout abominable things, swearing and screaming, and even spitting on the prime minister. Rabin didn't change his pace or his expression; he walked past it all, head held high, giving off the aura of a man of conviction, a man too busy in his pursuit to be swayed by such vile behavior. He showed extraordinary courage in those dark days, refusing to back down no matter the personal price. In the months that would follow, I never saw him once cancel a meeting or appearance—indeed, I never saw him give up any ground to the forces of hatred. He simply carried on.

As violence at home continued to drain support for the peace process, Rabin feared that if elections were held, we were likely to lose. Recognizing that we had to recapture the enthusiasm for peace, and tamp down the preference for war, I suggested we hold a grand rally—a peace rally, one that would give us the chance to show the Israeli people that though the voices of peace were being drowned out by the shouting fury of the opposition, they hadn't disappeared. Indeed, I believed that a peace rally had the power to draw those out who were afraid to raise their voices, encouraging more to do the same, which in turn could create a hopeful energy that would reverberate throughout the country. It could convince the people to believe again in the beauty and power of the future we were trying to make possible.

Rabin was anxious about the idea. "Shimon, what if it's a failure?" he asked me in a late-night call a few evenings after we first discussed the idea. "What if the people don't come?"

"They will come," I promised him.

Rabin and I arrived at the rally on November 4, 1995, to find a scene beyond our wildest expectations. He was stunned to see more than a hundred thousand people, gathered together in peace, for peace, in what was then known as Kings of Israel Square.

"This is beautiful," he said to me, once we met up at the venue and took our place on the balcony of city hall, overlooking the rally. It was there that we were overcome by the crescendo of cheering below. In the reflecting pool beneath us there were young Israelis jumping and splashing, smiling and dancing, a gorgeous reminder of what we were fighting for: not our own future, but theirs.

Rabin had truly been taken by surprise. It was the happiest I'd ever seen him—possibly the happiest day of his life. Across so many decades of working together, I had never heard him sing. Now all of a sudden he was singing "Shir l'shalom," the song of peace, out of a songbook he held in his hand. Even at the height of our greatest achievements, Rabin had never hugged me. All of a sudden, he hugged me.

As our time at the event drew to an end, we got ready to leave. We were supposed to all go down together, but just before we planned to depart, members of the intelligence service came in to speak with us. They had credible information that there would be an attempt on our lives, and for security purposes they wanted to change the way we had planned to exit. The intelligence suggested that the attacker was Arab; nobody could have imagined a Jewish assassin. When we were ready to go, they wanted us to walk separately toward our cars. It was not the first time we had heard such a warning; we had gotten used to staying calm in such circumstances.

Our security teams returned a few moments later to let us know that the cars were ready and waiting below. They wanted me to exit first, followed by Rabin. Before I turned to walk down the stairs, I went over to find Rabin. He was still happy as a child. I told him I was to leave first, and that I looked forward to talking about this triumph the next day. He gave me another hug. "Thank you, Shimon. Thank you."

I started down the steps toward my car, as cheers continued to echo all around me. Before I entered my car, I looked back to see Rabin walking down the stairs about one hundred feet behind me. My security agent opened the car door for me, and as I bent down to get in I heard a sound that still wakes me some nights, all these years later—the sound, in quick succession, of three shots being fired.

I tried to stand back up. "What happened?" I shouted to the security guard. But instead of answering me, he pushed me into the car and slammed the door as the car screeched off into the distance.

"What happened?" I demanded of the security officer who was driving. "What happened?"

They drove silently to the headquarters of Israel's Security Agency and ushered me inside, ignoring my demands for an answer. "Where's Rabin?" I insisted once we finally arrived. "Tell me what has happened."

It was then that I heard that there had been an attempt on his life. That he had been shot. That he had been taken to the hospital. But how severe the injuries, no one could say.

"Where is the hospital?" I demanded. "I am going there right now."

"You can't go there," said one of the security officers. "Your life is still in danger. We cannot let you go back out."

"You can talk of danger all you want," I said. "If you don't drive me there, I will go there by foot." Realizing they had little choice in the matter, the security officers obliged and drove me swiftly to the hospital. When I arrived, no one knew if Rabin was still with us. A crowd had gathered outside the hospital, weeping, fearing the worst, praying for a miracle.

"Where is he? What happened to him?" I asked of the first hospital staff I could see. No one had an answer—just tears in their eyes. "Take me to him!" I shouted. In all of the commotion, the head of the hospital saw me, and I him, and suddenly we were rushing toward each other.

"Tell me what has happened. Please."

"Mr. Peres," he said, with a crack in his voice, "I am sorry to have to say, the prime minister is dead."

It was like someone had attacked me with a knife, my chest laid bare, my heart punctured. I had forgotten how to breathe. I had just seen Rabin's face, smiling like I'd never seen before. There was so much life in him, so much hope and promise. And now "Shir l'shalom," our song for peace, was quite literally stained with blood—in the pages of the songbook Rabin was holding when attacked. The future we had fought for was suddenly so uncertain. How could it be that he was gone?

I turned and walked away from the doctor with a ringing in my ears, like a bomb had gone off, like I was surrounded by the chaos of war. Down the hallway I saw Leah, Rabin's wife, standing at the epicenter of an unimaginable tragedy. I could see that she had been told the words I could not imagine Sonia having to hear: the worst is true.

Leah and I went together to say a final farewell. He had a smile on his face—the face of a happy man, in total rest. Leah approached him and kissed him one last time. Then I went up to him. In wrenching sorrow, I kissed his forehead and said good-bye.

I was so distraught that I could barely speak when the minister of justice came to me.

"We have to appoint someone prime minister, immediately," he said. "It cannot wait. We cannot leave the ship without a captain. Especially not now."

"When? What?" It was all I could muster.

"We will nominate you," he said. "We're convening an emergency cabinet meeting. We must leave the hospital and go there right now."

We gathered together, holding a makeshift memorial for our fallen brother. All of the ministers agreed that I should take over as prime minister, voting on the spot to name me Rabin's successor. It was the most alone I had ever felt.

We were a nation in shock, not only because our prime minister had been killed, but because of the man who had done the killing. He was an Israeli, a Jew—one of our own, an extremist so deluded and desperate to halt our progress toward peace that his cowardly murder of a national hero was a source of pride and satisfaction. His action—and the depraved enthusiasm of the group of fanatics who agreed with him—was beyond anything we could have conjured in the depths of our nightmares. All at once it was maddening and confounding and impossibly painful.

At times of great sorrow, we lean on each other, and so it was for nearly every Israeli. There were spontaneous demonstrations, not of protest, but of love, as thousands took to the street in vigil, lighting candles on behalf of our fallen leader. I felt as though the weight of an entire nation were now resting on my shoulders.

Rabin and I had been great rivals for decades, but had become great partners in recent years. As I said after he passed, it sometimes happens in life that if you are two, you are more than two. If you are one, then you are less than one. I was so much less than one without him. Without warning he was gone and I had inherited a country in turmoil. If I acted incorrectly, I feared civil war. How could I be tough on those who supported the assassination without fanning such dangerous flames? I had so many decisions to make, and so quickly, and the only advice I wanted was his. I was tortured by his silence. When I returned to the prime minister's office, I couldn't bring myself to sit in his chair.

But I moved forward, in his honor and on behalf of the vision for peace we had shared. There was still work to be done, a country to heal, a peace process to save, a generation of children on both sides of our borders, to whom we owed a future made better than our past. With so much at stake, I knew I had but one choice: to set the terms of the national agenda, and to make the hard decisions that leadership demands.

. . .

The year 2016 marks twenty years since the end of my time as prime minister. When I had first taken the prime minister-ship after Rabin's death, Israel was more unified than at any other time in recent memory—not because there was sudden consensus about difficult and divisive issues, but because the loss of Rabin had been such a painful collective blow. As the country mourned, Israelis rallied around each other and closed ranks in support of their new prime minister. Many of the senior leaders in the Labor Party tried to convince me to call an early election. They argued that we were occupying a narrow window in which Labor could maintain its governing majority in the Knesset. Before Rabin's as-sassination, the conventional wisdom was that Labor would lose the next election because of the terror attacks. But now, in this moment of national unity, I was sure to win easily, and we were sure to remain in power.

I understood the political logic to their argument. It was clear and persuasive. But I did not see the decision as a political choice; to me it was a moral one. To call an early election was to choose to win power using the spilled blood of Rabin. There was no reality, political or otherwise, in which I would use his death that way.

Instead, I turned back to the work of peace, without Rabin by my side, but with his spirit in my heart. The second stage of the Palestinian negotiations had yet to be completed and, meanwhile, I had already sent Uri Savir to Syria to begin peace negotiations with Assad's government under my direction. And because terrorism had become such a terrible impediment to peace, I organized an international conference in Sharm el-Sheikh, where world leaders could discuss strategies to fight back against the threat. It was a hard and lonely time for me. My own party was frustrated that I hadn't called an election. My opponents were criticizing me daily, accusing me of being an appeaser, demanding military actions that would surely kill the peace process. Hamas and Islamic Jihad were meanwhile launching attacks on Israeli citizens. In early 1996, there were five gruesome terrorist attacks in Israel, one after the other, each seemingly worse than the next.

Indeed, the week that the bombings began was the worst of my life. When I visited the site of the first terrorist attack in Jerusalem, I stood before a mangled and melted bus that, just hours earlier, had been transporting everyday people on City Line 18. It looked like the carcass of a slain beast, covered in glass and char and blood. I was too transfixed by the horror of the scene to hear the gathered crowd booing me. "Peres is a murderer!" someone shouted. "Peres is next!" screamed another. I told Arafat that terrorism was strangling the prospects for peace, while he professed to having no power to stop it. "I don't think you understand what's at stake. If you do not unite your people under one rule," I warned, "the Palestinians will never have a state." Still, the bombings continued. A suicide bombing in Ashkelon. Another at the Purim Festival in Tel Aviv. I went to each site, over the objections of my security team and staff. I felt it was my obligation as prime minister to be there, both for those who had perished and been wounded, and for my country, which needed to be seen by the world as the resilient place it had always been. But when I stood there in Tel Aviv, my home for so long, and saw its streets burned and bloodied at what was supposed to be a joyful festival, I realized that despite my hopes, the environment for peace had grown increasingly untenable in the short term. When elections were held in May of that year, Benjamin Netanyahu prevailed in what was a deeply painful defeat for me. Out of nearly three million votes cast, he won by a margin of fewer than thirty thousand votes—yet it was still enough to drive the Likud party to power and put an end to the chapter Rabin and I had written together.

In the years to follow, there were still attempts to make peace, but the new context made it harder. In time the lifeblood of Oslo was drained, the framework largely discarded. And yet, its legacy remains. We fell short of our grandest ambitions—a permanent solution, a permanent peace—but the work was the beginning of a revolution, a defining moment that produced the foundation for a greater peace to come. It was this effort that gave us the two-state solution—the only framework that has a real chance to succeed. Because of our negotiations with the Palestinians, we still today have a camp of Palestinians, led by Mahmoud Abbas, who seek genuine peace. Without him, we would have only Hamas. Because of our negotiations, we were able to lay the groundwork and the framework for future agreement. An acknowledgment among Palestinians that it is 1967 borders, and not 1947 borders, that are the basis for discussion is in itself a kind of revolution in thinking. Without Oslo, we wouldn't have been able to open embassies and build relationships with former enemies, nor would we have been able to make peace with Jordan. Oslo allowed us to direct government investments into infrastructure and social programs. It opened up Israel's economy to the broader Middle East, and the broader Middle East's to Israel, allowing us to sign agreements and form partnerships that boosted our growth. And it is worth remembering that every subsequent Israeli government, even those that have not chosen peace as a priority, eventually adopted our framework, acknowledging that the only way to put an end to the vicious cycle of violence and terrorism is through peace—through two states, not one.

And yet there continues to be great skepticism about peace—not only whether it's possible, but whether it's even desirable. To the first question, I believe that peace is not only possible, but inevitable. The optimism I feel is a function not just of my identity, but of history. History, after all, is a powerful antidote to a cynical view of the world. How many times has it surprised us? How many times has it led us to realities that far exceeded our dreams? Who would have dreamed, after World War II, that just three years later, France, Germany, and Italy would join together in peaceful alliance? How many times did I hear experts tell us that lasting peace with Egypt and Jordan was simply impossible? How many times did the pessimists shake their head at the idea that among the Palestinians there would ever rise a broad constituency against terror?

We have seen the impossible made real again and again. There was a time when the Arab League subscribed to the Khartoum Formula, known as the three "no's": never make peace with Israel; never recognize Israel; never negotiate with Israel. Most of the people I worked with most of my life would never have imagined a time when the Arab League would publish an initiative that refutes them all. Never would they have believed that Arab leaders would speak out in favor of peace and against terror, not just abroad, but at home, or that Palestinians would recognize Israel within its 1967 borders. And yet peace, stubbornly, doggedly, finds a way, without consideration of the doubts of the experts.

I believe in the inevitability of peace because I understand the necessity of peace. Necessity is, perhaps, the most powerful concept of all. It is what drove the pioneers to settle the land. It is what pushed them to think creatively—to turn salted dirt into fertile ground, and transform a fallow desert into a community that could bear fruit. It was necessity that sent Ben-Gurion on a mission to build the IDF, to protect us at a time of our greatest vulnerability from the certainty of impending war. It was necessity that called upon Israeli leadership to build the impossible in Dimona, and to risk everything in Entebbe. And likewise, it will be the necessity of peace that brings it, finally—and fully—to fruition. The cost of hostility is simply too high.

I believe with all my being in the virtue of Zionism, and in the historic decision made by Ben-Gurion to accept the UN resolution for a partitioned Palestine. Even then, Ben-Gurion understood that in order to retain the Jewish character of our state, we had to uphold our values, and that our values are fundamentally democratic. Jews are taught that we are all born in the image of God. To believe this fundamental tenet, a Jewish state must embrace democracy, which demands full equality between the Jews and non-Jews. Democracy, after all, is not only the right of every citizen to be equal, but also the equal right of every citizen to be different. The future of the Zionist project depends on our embrace of the two-state solution. The danger, if Israel abandons this goal, is that the Palestinians will eventually accept a one-state solution. Because of demographics, this will leave us with a choice: stay Jewish or stay democratic. But it really isn't a choice at all. To lose our Jewish majority is to lose our Jewish character. To give up on democracy is to abandon our Jewish values. We must hold on to our values. We didn't give up our values even when we were facing furnaces and gas chambers. We lived as Jews and died as Jews and rose again as free Jewish people. We didn't survive merely to be a passing shadow in history, but as a new genesis, a nation intent on *tikkun olam,* on making the world aright.

In 1996, I established the Peres Center for Peace and Innovation because of my belief in people and their ability to bring positive change, and in recognition that peace cannot solely be made by governments; it must be made between people—between Jews and Arabs. And I have worked over the past twenty years to build those bonds through peace education, business partnerships, agriculture, and health care. But a permanent solution will require the reasoned wisdom of governments—ours and our neighbors. It will require leaders who understand that Israel is strong enough to make peace, and that making peace from a position of strength is imperative. To wait is to guarantee that the agreement will be worse than any we have ever considered; Israel will be negotiating, for the very first time, from a position of weakness. In a reality where immediate peace is the only way to save Zionism, the Palestinian negotiators will hold all the cards.

The question, then, is not whether we will achieve peace, but when, and at what cost, knowing that the longer we wait, the higher it grows. This is why I see grave danger in giving in to skepticism at a time when we should be redoubling our efforts. In history, there is no reverse gear.

As I know far too well, achieving peace is not easy. But there is no alternative but to return to the table. The yesterday between us and the Palestinians is full of sadness. I believe that the Israel and Palestine of tomorrow can offer our children a new ray of hope. The advancement of peace will complete the march of Israel toward the fulfillment of its founding vision: an exemplary and thriving country, living in peace and security in its homeland and among its neighbors.

It has been more than twenty years since I stood on a stage in Oslo and alongside Rabin and Arafat accepted the Nobel Peace Prize. Much has changed since then, but my core message remains unaltered: countries can no longer afford to divide the world into friend and foe. Our foes are now universal—poverty and famine, radicalization and terror. These know no borders and threaten all nations. And so we must act swiftly to build the bonds of peace, to tear down walls built with bitterness and animosity, so that we can together confront the challenges and seize the opportunities of a new era.

Optimism and naïveté are not one and the same. That I am optimistic does not mean I expect a peace of love; I expect, simply, a peace of necessity. I do not envision a perfect peace, but I believe we can find a peace that allows us to live side by side without the threat of violence.

In the years to come, we must remember that peace negotiations will never begin with a happy end. They will begin, instead, from an obscure, complicated situation, colored with memories of pain and of violence. And they will take time. So let us rededicate ourselves to that effort, and save the happy end for the ending. I believe with all my heart in the vision of the prophets, the vision of peace, for the country I love so much. And what I know to be true is that a majority of people on both sides of the divide are eager for peace—especially the young generation. They are the ones who transform the impossible into the unlikely, the ones whose creativity and passion will turn the unlikely into reality. Whether the leaders catch up to the young, or the young become the leaders, we are inevitably walking in the same direction. The road will be littered with obstacles. But it remains the only one worth traveling.

EPILOGUE

In the span of my lifetime, I have seen the extraordinary: During my childhood, I rode in horse-drawn carriages in Vishneva. During my presidency, I witnessed the birth of the self-driving car. I have seen technology that sent men to the moon and vaccines that have eradicated deadly diseases from the face of the earth. I have seen billions lifted out of poverty, a world still in conflict but more peaceful than at any point of human existence. And I have seen the Jewish people fight for a thin slice of desert, then transform it into a country that surpassed our grandest dreams.

I recognize that progress has not always been steady. It is often uneven, with tragic steps backward. The Allied powers defeated the Nazis and made the world safe for democracy—but not before the deaths of millions. The splitting of the atom created the potential for new energy and new sciences—but with it came the heavy fear that a push of a button would bring global catastrophe. The Internet has allowed billions of people to break free from old dogmas—but it has also allowed the forces of evil to spread hate in an instant. We have seen the danger when technology and morality do not coexist.

At the time of this writing, we face new dangers. A decline in tolerance. A rise in nationalism. A world at the height of prosperity that is not widely shared, where we see rising inequality, both within countries and between them. And yet in spite of these forces, I remain optimistic. Not only because it is my nature, but because I can see the countervailing winds blowing in the direction of progress. We are in transition—from one era to another. It is not humanity's first, but it is its most rapid and comprehensive. It is the leap from the age of territory to the age of science.

The age of territory was driven by acquisition. Leaders of nations sought to increase their nation's power by gaining territory—mostly through force. Accumulated military prowess by one drove would-be victims to arm. War was thus inevitable. Lost lives and wasted resources were its currency. And always, one side's gain was the other's loss. Today, the importance of land as the primary source of human livelihood has diminished, giving way to science instead. Unlike territory, science has no borders or flags. Science can't be conquered by tanks or defended by fighter jets. It has no limitations. A nation can increase its scientific achievement without taking anything from somebody else. In fact, great scientific achievement by one nation lifts the fortunes of all nations. It is the first time in history that we can win, without making anyone lose.

In the age of science, the traditional power of states and leaders is declining. Rather than politicians, it is innovators that drive the global economy and wield the most influence. The young leaders who created Facebook and Google have sparked a revolution without killing one person. The globalized economy affects every state, yet no single state is powerful enough to determine outcomes. We are participating in the birth of a new world.

Past discoveries have proven the power of science. When my grandfather was in the prime of his life, for example, someone with a tooth infection would have no recourse, only terrible pain and probable death. Today antibiotics allow us to live better lives than the royalty of the recent past. The high-tech revolution may be just as profound.

We have already seen the power of mobile technology to break down even the harshest of dictatorships. While governments can try to restrict free expression, they increasingly and inevitably fail. In the Middle East, there are nearly 130 million boys and girls with smartphones. They may not be able to break free from their government, but with new access to new knowledge, they can break free from the old ideology. We may soon find that peace is made possible not through negotiation but through innovation.

Technological progress has created bridges across borders and languages and cultures. We have yet to fully comprehend the opportunities that will continue to grow from this transformational interconnectivity. Yet transformations, however worthy, do not follow a clear path. One cannot forge connections without the prior existence of gaps, but one also cannot forge connections if those gaps are too wide. In today's world, the separation between generations is wider than the separation between nations, and it is the young who now hold the power to create greater global impact than statesmen and generals ever could. Those firmly planted in the past will surely resist the future. Today, the Middle East is ailing. The malady stems from pervasive violence; from shortages of food, water, and educational opportunities; from discrimination against women; and more virulently, from the absence of freedom.

Too many in our region are lingering on the old idea of territory as might. We are still witness to horrific wars perpetrated by governments of the old order, those who prefer to remember than to dream. Nonetheless the trend is unmistakable: wars are gradually being rendered futile. They have already lost their rational motivation and their moral justification. And though despots have the power to kill thousands, they do not have the power to kill an idea.

The imperative of the young generation is to help complete this transformation. We need a generation that sees leadership as a noble cause, defined not by personal ambition, but by morality— and a call to service. We need leaders who believe that the world can be changed not by killing and shooting but by creating and competing, leaders who prefer to be controversial for the right reasons, rather than popular for the wrong ones, leaders who use their imagination more than their memory. I am filled with hope because I believe we have that generation at hand, walking the earth at this very moment. To the young people of the world, I hope that you will take to heart what David Ben-Gurion taught me. It was from him I learned that the vision of the future should shape the agenda for the present; that one can overcome obstacles by dint of faith; that there is nothing more responsible than to take risks today for the sake of tomorrow's chance; that just as birth requires the pain of labor, success requires the pain of failure.

I don't expect you to take the word of an old man; if I have earned the title of expert, it is only on what was. There is no expert on what will be. And yet, without knowing the future, I remain a man full of hope. Hope for peace. Hope that we will continue to make the Promised Land a land of promise. Hope that Israel will uphold social justice as a moral country. Hope that we will raise our eyes to the realized dreams of our prophets, who showed us that liberty is also the soul of the Jewish heritage. My greatest hope is that our children, like our forefathers, will continue to plow the historical Jewish furrow in the field of the human spirit; that Israel will become the center of our heritage, not merely our homeland; and that the Jewish people will both be inspired by others and a continued source of inspiration.

I am grateful that the chapters of my life are entwined with the birth and construction of Israel. I will be forever indebted to Ben-Gurion, who called me to work for him, and who gave me the wonderful privilege of serving my country. For nearly seventy years, inspired by his leadership, I tried to gather strength for Israel, to build its defense and pursue peace for my people—our heart's truest desire. I love this country—the scent of the orange blossoms in the spring; the hum of the Jordan River; the silent peace of the Negev nights; and always, its people, who at every encounter of my life have proved valiant and faithful and generous and resilient.

I do not pretend that I am a complex individual. I was given my life, some two and a half billion seconds: I did some reckoning, and I decided to do something with those seconds so that I might make a difference. I think I decided correctly. I don't regret any of my dreams. My only regret is not having dreamed more. I got my life as a gift. I'll give it up without an overdraft.

Every once in a while, someone will ask me to look back on my career and identify the achievement in my life of which I am proudest. I respond by telling them the story of a great painter, who was once approached by an admirer of his art.

"Which of your paintings do you consider your most beautiful?" the man asked.

The painter looked up at the man, then turned his gaze toward a large blank canvas, resting on an easel in the corner of the room.

"The one I will paint tomorrow," he replied.

My answer is the same.

—September 2016

AFTERWORD

On September 13, 2016, Shimon Peres met with hundreds of entrepreneurs from all over the world and encouraged them to invest in Israeli technologies. He was joined by his son, Chemi, who interviewed him onstage. Peres also launched a social media campaign that day to bolster Israeli industries. Before the day was over, he was being rushed to the hospital.

Shimon Peres died on September 28, 2016. Thousands of people, including leaders from dozens of countries, came together to pay their respects.

At a special cabinet meeting in memoriam that morning, Prime Minister Netanyahu observed that it was "the first day of the State of Israel without Shimon Peres."

The Israeli Innovation Center will open in 2018. The Peres Center for Peace and Innovation will continue his important work, on his behalf, and on behalf of all those who seek a more peaceful and prosperous world.